Write It Down, Make it Happen

WRITE IT DOWN, MAKE IT HAPPEN

KNOWING WHAT YOU WANT—
AND GETTING IT!

Henriette Anne Klauser, Ph.D.

SIMON & SCHUSTER
A VIACOM COMPANY

First published in Great Britain by Simon & Schuster UK Ltd, 2001
A Viacom Company

Copyright © Henriette Anne Klauser, 2001

1 3 5 7 9 10 8 6 4 2

Simon & Schuster UK Ltd
Africa House
64–78 Kingsway
London WC2B 6AH

Simon & Schuster Australia
Sydney

A CIP catalogue record for this book is available from the
British Library

ISBN 0-7432-0938-9

Typeset in 11/15 Bembo by
Palimpsest Book Production Limited,
Polmont, Stirlingshire.
Printed and bound in Finland by WS Bookwell

To Dorothy and Bill Harrison,
whose love for each other and their children
spills over to embrace the world.

I find my shelter in you.

I worked for a menial's hire,
Only to learn, dismayed,
That any wage I had asked of Life,
Life would have willingly paid.

—ANONYMOUS POET,
quoted by Napoleon Hill in
Think and Grow Rich

CONTENTS

WRITE IT DOWN, MAKE IT HAPPEN

INTRODUCTION

An Egyptian scribe sits on my fireplace hearth. The stone statue is a replica brought back from my trip to Cairo several years ago. He sits cross-legged, a papyrus scroll across his lap and a stylus poised in his hand, ready to write. His eyes are wise and faraway, as though he could see the future. He is a symbol of what this book is all about.

For the ancient people of the Nile, writing something made it real.

Think Big – It Works!

In the 1920s and 30s, a host of titles appeared exclaiming (sometimes literally: Victory!!! Success!!! You can do it!!!) the wonders of the 'science of thought': Napoleon Hill's *Think and Grow Rich*, Claude M. Bristol's *The Magic of Believing*, James Allen's *As a Man Thinketh*, and then, in the 50s, David J. Schwartz's *The Magic of Thinking Big*.

Remarkably, all of these books are still in print and readily available at the bookstore now, fifty, sixty, even seventy years later. As archaic the language, quaint the examples and blatant the sexism seem today, these books still hit a resonant chord with a modern audience.

One small pamphlet, written in 1926 and still circulating over a million and a half copies later, is simply called *It Works!* by RHJ. This tiny tome sums up the staying power of these proponents of proactive, positive thinking. More than just a glossed-over, Pollyannaish, witless approach, they have an important message, which *It Works!* puts succinctly in its opening epigram:

IF YOU KNOW WHAT YOU WANT, YOU CAN HAVE IT.

All our years of brain research, all our current knowledge about the corpus callosum, the reticular activating system, and the workings of the human mind, and we are still left with an 'oh wow' sense of wonder that 'it works'.

Write It Down, Make It Happen keeps that sense of wonder and is grounded in the same now-scientific truth – that setting your intent, focusing on the outcome, being clear about what you want in life can make your dreams come true.

There is another key element that comes into play, an element that each and every one of these long-lasting books has in common: The first step in all of them is to write down your goal.

Celebrity Stories

I keep hearing wonderful stories about celebrities who, before they were as famous as they are today, wrote down their dreams.

Jim Carrey walked up to the Hollywood Hills and wrote a cheque to himself for ten million dollars. On the memo line, he wrote, 'For Services Rendered'. For years, the comedian carried the cheque around with him, long before he was ever paid that kind of money for a movie. Now he is one of the highest-paid entertainers in the industry, getting twenty million dollars for a film. In a touching gesture, Carrey tucked the visionary cheque into his dad's jacket pocket before they buried him.

Scott Adams, creator of the comic *Dilbert*, has a whole string of writing-down dreams that came true, one step at a time. Adams says that when you write down a goal, 'you'll observe things happening that will make that objective more likely to materialize.'

As a lowly technology worker in a cubicle in corporate America, Adams kept doodling at his office desk. Then he began to write, fifteen times a day, 'I will become a syndicated cartoonist.'

Through many rejections, he persevered and finally it happened: he signed a contract for his strip to be syndicated. That's when he started writing, 'I will be the best cartoonist on the planet.'

How to judge that?

Well, *Dilbert* is syndicated in almost 2,000 newspapers worldwide. The Dilbert Zone website gets 100,000 visitors a day. Adams's first book, *The Dilbert Principle*, sold more than

1.3 million copies. Products from mousepads to coffee cups to desk calendars based on the *Dilbert* characters are everywhere, and there is even a weekly TV show.

Now Scott Adams writes fifteen times a day, 'I will win a Pulitzer Prize.'

Suze Orman, financial wizard, author of the number one *New York Times* bestseller, *The 9 Steps to Financial Freedom*, and a frequent guest on *Oprah*, tells how she started out. She got a job at Merrill Lynch and was terrified she would not be able to meet her sales quota. The most she had ever made up until then was four hundred dollars a month as a waitress.

'I created what I wanted for myself first on paper. Every morning before I went to work, I would write over and over again: "I am young, powerful and successful, producing at least $10,000 a month."'

Even after surpassing that target figure, she continued to carry the saying around with her 'like a lucky charm in words. I replaced the message of fear and my belief I was inadequate with a message of endless possibility.'

And writing down her new truth helped make it materialize.

My own inspiration for this book came from closer to home. My son Peter at the age of twelve came to me one day with a perplexed expression on his face and a piece of paper in his hand.

'I found this list from two years ago when I was cleaning my room. I don't know how, but everything on this list came true, and I forgot I wrote it.'

Among other things, he had taken karate lessons, tried out for a play, slept overnight at the park, and got a bird – all without being conscious of checking off items on the forgotten list.

Peter's experience made me think. I noticed the same phenomenon happening in my own life.

In one exciting and memorable week of my life, I managed to autograph books on Broadway in New York City, go backstage at the Metropolitan Opera, be interviewed on the radio for an audience of several million and hear Plácido Domingo live in a full-length opera. It wasn't until I got back to the West Coast that I found, like Peter before me, an old goals list I had forgotten about.

All of the things I had just accomplished were on that list.

I tell the story of Peter's list and my list in a chapter of my book *Put Your Heart on Paper*. Another chapter in that book, 'The Shoeless Joe Principle', treats synchronicity, or what seems like coincidence, quoting the line from the film *Field of Dreams*, 'If you build it, he will come.' Building it before he gets there is stepping out in faith, just as writing it down says you believe that it's attainable.

Those two chapters were the beginning of my investigation into the power of writing things down to make them happen, and the genesis of this book.

Who Am I to Tell You This?

Let me tell you a bit about my background.

I have a Ph.D. in English literature and have taught in universities in New York, Los Angeles, Seattle and Lethbridge, Alberta, in Canada. My first book, *Writing on Both Sides of the Brain*, addresses the problems of procrastination and deals with writing anxiety. It is about learning to separate the writing from the editing. It teaches you first to write, then to polish your words, rather than trying to do both at the same time. *Writing on Both Sides of the Brain* describes how to interview the Critic, that inner carping voice that can hold you back, and introduces the concept of Rapidwriting, writing fast, lickety-split, past the Critic.

For the past fifteen years, I have been giving workshops around the world and presentations at national associations. It was out of that work that my second book, *Put Your Heart on Paper*, evolved. Once people grasped and used the concepts of fluent writing I taught them, they would often say to me, 'This isn't about writing; it's about life.' *Put Your Heart on Paper* applies the freedom to write to relationships and shows how to stay connected in this loose-ends world. Two of the concepts in that work that I explore further here are 'Writing Through to Resolution', (see chapter 6) and how to let writing help you think (see chapter 2).

Where Do These Stories Come From?

Once I decided to write this book, the stories to go in it seemed to seek me out, in much the same manner that readers of this book will find the world cooperating with them. How could it not be so? A book *about* adventures happening has to *be* an adventure happening. Stories came up and tapped me on the shoulder; every phone call was loaded. Nine of the people whose stories I tell here I did not even *know* when I proposed the idea to the publisher.

One of those people was the bestselling writer Elaine St James. It was she who called me, on the recommendation of a mutual friend, about something else. The interview I had with her blew my socks off. I was so wound up after talking to her, I could hardly sit still – what was it that turned me on and spun me around and around? First, it was Elaine herself – a high-energy person. She made giant leaps sound so possible, so near and accessible (and she was *funny*). Further, in talking to her, I had a clear vision that her story would be an important piece in *Write It Down, Make It Happen.* Not one, but two chapters came from that conversation (see chapters 17 and 18). As I put those chapters together, I realized with a start that *they weren't there a week ago.*

That's the part that thrilled me most: how readily what I needed was available to me. The 'Work' fleshed itself out even as I wrote it.

Write It Down, Make It Happen was written almost entirely in the coffee-houses of Seattle; several of the stories come right out of this penchant I have for writing in the middle of things. For example, the story of Jaimée's demo tape in chapter 20, and Maria's dream apartment in chapter 8. When you write in a café, life keeps happening all around you.

And then, of course, I followed my own dictum and simply wrote it down when I needed a good story.

For example, as I was gathering together the anecdotes to illustrate the principles of this book, I noticed something was missing. I wanted to show that my techniques could work wherever in the world you were. One morning I wrote,

> *I need a rural story. I want my readers to know that these techniques work for everyone whether you live in a big city or a small town.*

Two days later, my office phone rang. A woman named Marian was calling from Wells, Nevada (population 1,000). She had read my other books and wanted to know if I ever came to Nevada to do workshops. We got to talking, and soon she was telling me a remarkable narrative about an impossible dream come true – and wouldn't you know, she wrote it down before it happened. Marian's touching tale became the impetus for chapter 14, 'Taking the Initiative'.

How to Approach This Book

Some people keep journals; some jot down ideas on napkins, the backs of envelopes, pages torn from a legal pad, or any scrap paper near at hand. Do not fret about the kind of paper to use to write it down, or worry whether it should be bound in a notebook or loose on stationery. Any kind of paper, lined or unlined, quality or coarse, in a notebook or out of it, and any kind of pen – or pencil – with any colour ink will do. My only rule is *date* whatever you write down. (You can wear whatever you choose. There is no dress code.)

Maybe you are beginning to get the general idea. This is not a contest, where you are disqualified unless you print legibly, follow the rules, write on an index card, and remember to include the boxtop. You can write it down any way you want and still have results. Jim Carrey wrote it once and put it in his pocket; Scott Adams and Suze Orman wrote it over and over daily; my son Peter wrote it and lost it. My point is that *any*body can do this and there is no right way or wrong way, because everyone does it differently, and it still works.

It's a Matter of Faith

I saw a bumper sticker with a catchy slogan on a car in the church car park. I copied it onto the back of the Sunday bulletin so I'd remember it. It said, 'Good Happens'.

It made me smile to see that sign.

'Good happens' is the philosophy behind this book – my premise is the overriding belief that good things happen and that life is a narrative you have a hand in writing.

We get so hung up on format, but it's the faith that matters, the faith that 'good happens'.

Have you heard of the practice of burying a statue of St Joseph head-first in your garden when you want to sell your house quickly?

Many people I know swear by it, and even respected national newspapers have done articles describing the pious practice.

When I was preparing to sell my house, I hated the thought of keeping it in showroom condition, down to monitoring toothpaste flecks on the bathroom mirrors. I cringed at the idea of strangers traipsing through my personal rooms. Somewhat sheepishly, I went to the local Catholic gift shop, For Heaven's Sake, to buy a statue of St Joseph.

When I told Agnes, the proprietor, what I wanted, she added an element I had not heard of up until then. Agnes said that you need to put a marker where you plant St Joseph, so after the house sells, you can dig him up and put him in a place of honour in your new home.

I started to ask Agnes all kinds of questions. I was worried about doing it 'right'.

Did the statue have to be an expensive one, carved of wood and handpainted, or would a cheaper small model, a moulded plastic figurine work as well? Which way did I face him, towards the house or the street? Do I plant him in the back or the front garden? Would the sandbox be OK?

Frankly, I didn't have the heart to bury him. Would it still work if I protected him by wrapping him in cling film or putting him in a plastic bag? It seemed so crude to cover him in dirt, or was that earthy contact part of what was needed here? Did I have to get the statue blessed before or after, or not at all?

Agnes said, 'Look, you don't have to bury him at all, if you don't want. St Joseph is the patron saint of families and of homes. If you ask for his help, he will be there for you. It's not the burying that does it, it's the prayer to St Joseph, and the confidence that he will help you.'

I liked what Agnes was telling me.

I put a small polymer statue of St Joseph on a glass shelf on the étagère as you enter the house, next to a triptych of the Madonna and a statue of the goddess Kuan Yin that has been in my family for three generations. On a shelf below sat a little replica of Selkit, who guarded King Tut's tomb.

Open House was scheduled for Sunday. In preparation, the estate agent hammered a 'For Sale' sign into the lawn. Early viewing was to begin on Thursday. I dreaded it.

I knew what I wanted, as impossible as it seemed. I wanted my house to sell quickly – without going on the market.

It was Wednesday morning when I put St Joseph on the étagère, and then left to take my daughter Katherine to the orthodontist. While in the dentist's waiting room, I described in writing my perfect scenario. I wrote it as though it had already happened.

A woman in the neighbourhood, a complete stranger to me, found out that I was planning to put my house on the market. Wednesday afternoon she came by with her husband and bought the house for over the listing price, and I never had to show it at all.

I wrote those exact words in my big, bound notebook on Wednesday morning. Wednesday night, it happened precisely as I pictured it, with a nifty difference. While the woman was viewing the house, two other couples drove by and asked to take a look around. Within the hour, all *three* parties had drawn up papers, returned with their estate agents, and made offers on the house above the asking price.

The small, cream-coloured St Joseph sat in a place of honour on the kitchen table as we negotiated the various contracts and chose the best buyer.

By midnight Wednesday, I had sold my house. And I never had to show it at all.

THERE IS no right way or wrong way to do it.
Life is a narrative that you have a hand in writing.
Let's begin.

List of Questions

Here are some thoughts that might be running through your head:

- I hate to write. How is this kind of writing different? (See chapter 1.)
- I don't know what I want. (See Marc's Story, chapter 2.)
- What if? What if? What if? What if I don't get what I want? What if I *do*? I'm scared. (See Janine's Story, chapter 5.)
- How do I know the difference between wanting something and being ready to receive it? (See Gloria's Story, chapter 4.)
- Is there more than one way to get a certain goal? (See Outcome, chapter 8; Breakdown, chapter 20.)
- How do I know when I am on the right track? (See Watching for Signs and Signals, chapter 1.)
- Can I have more than one goal at a time? (See Stacking, chapter 12.)
- What do I do when I am stuck? (See Suggestion Box, chapter 3; Get Near Water, chapter 9; Getting Unstuck, chapter 6; Polishing Coconuts, chapter 1; Writing Letters to God, chapter 15.)
- Does it matter how specific I am? (See Sydne's Story, chapter 7.)
- How do I keep the dream alive? (See Focusing on the Outcome, chapter 8.)
- Does the support of others help or should I keep it to myself? (See The Seymour Group, chapter 13.)
- What is the difference between fantasy and imagination

in goal setting? (See Bill's Story, chapter 11.)

- Why am I afraid to dream big, to ask for what I want? (See Marc's Story, chapter 2.)
- What if I write it down and it does not happen? (See Handling Breakdown, chapter 20.)
- What do I need to do to complete the cycle? (See Giving Thanks, chapter 19.)

The chapters that follow answer these concerns and tell the stories of people who have put the book's principles to good use, each in his or her own unique way. They are extraordinary, ordinary people, just like you. The people in these pages have told their stories not so you'll think they are wonderful, but so you know that you are. By the time you have finished reading this book and doing the exercises, you will know how to write it down and make it happen in your own life.

1

TE IT DOWN,

KE IT HAPPEN

Without further ado, before you read the chapters which follow, I want you to compose your own list of goals. Go to an espresso bar and buy a latte or put on a pot of peppermint tea at your own house. Set the stereo for the kind of music you like best and start to write.

Write fast. Do not linger over the page. If you find yourself dismissing a goal as grandiose or far-fetched, write it anyway and put a star next to it. That's a live one.

Do not be afraid of wanting too much. Write down even those ambitions which have no practical means of accomplishment.

Keep on writing. Write from your heart and make the list as long as you like.

Lou Holtz, the American football coach, did this in 1966. He was twenty-eight years old when he sat down at his dining room table and wrote out one hundred and seven impossible goals. He had just lost his job, he had no money in the bank, and his wife, Beth, was eight months pregnant with their third child. He was so discouraged that Beth gave him a copy of *The Magic of Thinking Big* by David J. Schwartz to help lift his spirits. Up until then, Holtz says, he was totally lacking in motivation.

'There are so many people, and I was one of them, who don't do anything special with their lives. The book said you should write down all the goals you wanted to achieve before you died.'

The goals he wrote in answer to that challenge were both personal and professional. Most seemed impossible to a twenty-eight-year-old out-of-work man. His list included having dinner at the White House, appearing on the *Tonight Show*, meeting the Pope, becoming head coach at Notre Dame, winning a national championship, being coach of the year, landing on an aircraft carrier, making a hole in one and jumping out of an aeroplane.

If you check out Coach Lou Holtz's website, along with this list you will get pictures – pictures of Holtz with the Pope, with President Ronald Reagan at the White House, joking around with Johnny Carson. In addition, a description of what it was like to jump out of an aeroplane and get not one but two holes in one.

Of the one hundred and seven goals on his list from 1966, Lou Holtz has achieved eighty-one.

So give yourself permission to dream, to be totally unrealistic. (Richard Bolles says, 'One of the saddest lines in the world is, "Oh, come now, be realistic".') Climb Mt Kilimanjaro. Endow a university or a hospital. Compose an opera. Start an orphanage. Become a better parent. Play the flute in the Albert Hall. Discover a cure for an untreatable disease. Get a patent. Appear on TV, or whatever equivalent grandiose schemes you can come up with – if money were no object and time were not a factor. Money is no object, and time is not a factor.

Make It Happen: Watching for Signs and Signals

Once you write a goal in good faith, how do you know you are on the right path? Signs are all around you – sometimes literally. My daughter Emily, running around Green Lake, spotted a young lad of about fourteen rollerblading with a sandwich board attached to his back and front:
FREE QUEEN-SIZE BED. FOLLOW ME.

Turns out his grandmother was moving and giving away a queen-size bed with mattress, headboard, springs and a dressing table to boot – perfect for Emily's friend who was looking for ways to furnish her new student apartment.

Emily lives her life in constant expectation of good things happening, and so they do. Emily knows that assistance is there for her whenever she needs it. Once, she was labouring over choosing a term paper theme at the downtown library, when a voice, as though from heaven, shattered the library silence:

'All students needing help with homework, please come to the second floor.'

She was the only student who answered the call – and had the head librarian all to herself in a conference room for exclusive and rewarding tutoring on her topic.

I have often wished that when we are struggling with a decision or dilemma that the clouds would part and a cosmic Charlton Heston-type voice would invite us to the second floor, where the Librarian of Life would sit with us for several hours, patiently answering all our questions and giving direction.

'ALL THOSE NEEDING HELP WITH LIFE, PLEASE COME TO THE SECOND FLOOR.'

FACT IS, there is that kind of direct and personal guidance available, but often we don't hear or see it.

Or, if we get the message at all, we dismiss it as accidental, which diminishes its personal nature. We think of such occurrences as 'coincidences' – isolated events that are easily chalked up to luck or happenstance. I prefer to call them 'Go! Incidences'. A 'Go! Incidence' is part of a pattern. Such events are a sign, a signal. 'Go! Incidences' carry the forward motion of a green light, the final-syllable urgency of a referee at the track: 'On your mark . . . get set . . . go!'

C. G. Jung called it 'synchronicity', when events coincide in a serendipitous way; some call it 'messages from the universe' or 'cosmic connections'. It is the sense that you are not alone, and that your life, no matter how it may seem at any particular disastrous moment, is part of a larger plan.

Some believe that we send out energy waves, transmissions, vibrations, whatever, that attract people, solutions, to us. Others call it 'divine intervention'. These views are not mutually exclusive – I, for one, hold a little bit of each of them.

What these views have in common is a duality that 1) puts us in charge, while 2) also implying a higher power who is guiding, watching out, caring about each and every one of us.

Writing it down sends a notice to the universe, 'Hey! I'm ready!' And 'Go! Incidences' are signs that send a message back: 'I got your signal, and I'm working on it.'

Help from Your Brain

Writing down your dreams and aspirations is like hanging up a sign that says, 'Open for Business'. Or, as my friend Elaine puts it, by writing it down, you declare yourself in the game. Putting it on paper alerts the part of your brain known as the reticular activating system to join you in the play.

At the base of the brain stem, about the size of a little finger, is a group of cells whose job it is to sort and evaluate incoming data. This control centre is known as the reticular activating system (RAS). The RAS sends the urgent stuff to the active part of your brain and sends the non-urgent to the subconscious. The RAS awakens the brain to consciousness and keeps it alert – just as surely as your baby's cry in the night, from all the way down the hall, can waken you from a deep sleep. The RAS evaluates the non-essential night-time noises – the dripping tap, the crickets, or neighbourhood traffic – and filters out the non-urgent, waking you up only for the urgent. The baby cries, and in a split second you are bolt upright in bed, wide awake and ready to rescue the infant in distress.

The keenest, most familiar example of the reticular activating system at work is an experience all of us have had at one time or another. You are in a packed room; you can barely hear the conversation of the person you are talking to above the din of the crowd.

Suddenly, someone clear on the other side of the room mentions *your name*. And that one word cuts through the sea of sound and your ears immediately perk up. You turn your head towards the speaker, eager now to tune in to the rest of what he or she is saying about you, straining to hear if it is good news, ready to defend against the bad.

That is a prime example of your monitoring mechanism, your reticular activating system, at work. You have just tuned in to something specific and useful to you.

Although you may think you are giving your conversational companion undivided attention, the fact is your attention is fragmented and subconsciously taking in the tower of babel around you, sorting, sorting, sorting, even as you speak. Your name when spoken stands out as prominently as a speck of gold in a miner's pan of gravel.

The RAS is like a filtering system of the brain. Writing it down sets up the filter. Things start to appear – it's a matter of activating your filtering system.

If you have never owned a Honda before, and you buy a blue Honda, all of a sudden you see blue Hondas all over town. You might wonder, Where are all these blue Hondas coming from? But they were there all along; you were just not paying attention to them.

Putting a goal in writing is like buying a blue Honda; it sets up a filter that helps you be aware of certain things in your surroundings. Writing triggers the RAS, which in turn sends a signal to the cerebral cortex: 'Wake up! Pay attention! Don't miss this detail!' Once you write down a goal, your brain will be working overtime to see you get it and will alert you to the signs and signals that, like the blue Honda, were there all along.

Polishing Coconuts

Often a goal, once written, will materialize without any further effort on your part. But it doesn't hurt either to 'prime the pump'. The more attractive you make whatever your ambition and the more you approach it in a spirit of fun, the more others will want to play along to make your dream a reality.

I call this playful spreading of the word 'polishing coconuts'.

Scientists in the 1960s were monitoring monkeys on a remote Japanese island who were cleaning sand off sweet potatoes by washing them in a stream. When the critical mass of monkeys doing this activity reached a certain number, primates on another island began doing the same thing. Ken Keyes Jr. took this experiment as a metaphor for an individual's personal responsibility to think peace. You never know if you might be the 'hundredth monkey' exploding the common consciousness into mass under-standing.

I use the expression 'polishing coconuts' (somehow it is more catchy than 'getting sand off yams') to mean how activity in one area generates movement in another. When you show your earnestness and intention by writing it down, something opens up. The word gets out.

My sons, James and Peter, own and operate a graphic design firm. They are imaginative, creative and indefatigable workers and their business is thriving. At the beginning of each month, they have a planning session where they write down their goals for the month. Then every Monday morning, they select and write on a blackboard the goals for the week. From that point on, they know that their activities − often indirectly − will feed those goals. What delights them constantly is the amount of work they get from untapped sources.

Peter and James are gleeful when they talk about the success they have 'polishing coconuts' − when they are wooing one account and another opens up from an unexpected place. Peter gives an example:

'We wanted to generate more business for Bullseye Graphics, so we put together a newsletter and sent it out to our existing clients. Almost immediately, we started getting phone calls, but interestingly enough, the phone calls weren't from clients; they were from people not on our mailing list. We were putting the energy out there and the phone started ringing – from new contacts.'

They wrote down the goal: *We want more exposure, to get our name before the public.* They set up a stand at a trade show; they sent notices out to area companies who might need design help; they approached new businesses with an introductory offer giving them a deal on an identity package. Many of these efforts and expenditures did not pan out directly, but what was totally unexpected and could not have been predicted was that one day they got a call from the *Wall Street Journal.* The *Wall Street Journal* was doing an article on successful small businesses and had been given their name by a local photocopy shop as two 'movers and shakers'. The article went out on the Internet and gave them all kinds of exposure.

Finding a Perfect Marketing Match

My friend Holly was interested in hiring someone to help her do a commercial. I told her to write down her goal and then I started 'polishing coconuts' for her on my little island. I called several fellow speakers for referrals and they in turn led me to some of the best in the industry. I contacted each of them, told them about Holly, and got good advice from all of them. Then I brainstormed some ideas with my pal John, who had just done a TV commercial, to get some tips from him to pass on to Holly.

When I called Holly back with all this information, she had hired someone – the perfect match had called her.

Did that mean my time was wasted, that I was of no help to her at all, because the answer came from a different quarter? Not at all. Bob McChesney, my friend and teacher, calls it, 'stirring the pot'.

Holly stirs up the pot by calling me; I stir up the pot for Holly, and her former publicist, who is now directing commercials, calls out of the blue and offers to help Holly do exactly what she needs. That's the way the world works and how the wheels are set in motion when you write down your goals.

'Polishing coconuts' creates a kind of Jungian synchron-icity, a convergence of meaningful events. Write it down to be clear in your commitment to its possibility and then activity *here* will create related movement *there*.

Write it down to make it happen.

You never know when your signal will be picked up on another island.

2

KNOWING
WHAT YOU WANT:
SETTING GOALS

What is the 'it' in 'write it down'?

When you don't have an answer to that question, when you don't know what your goals are, you can use your writing to point you in the right direction. If you don't know what you want, start writing. Writing makes its own meaning.

Marc's Story

Marc Acito and I first met at the Seattle Opera production of Puccini's *Turandot*, where he sang the part of the Chinese minister, Pong. When I told him about *Write It Down, Make It Happen*, my work in progress, he said that he had a good story to tell me, so I made an appointment to meet him at the apartment the opera company had rented for him in the Queen Anne neighbourhood. When I arrived, he made me some tea and put a crusty loaf of peasant bread and a dish of olive oil on the table. Then he sprinkled fresh Parmigiano Reggiano on top of the oil. He told me his story with great gusto and as he talked, he tore off chunks of bread and dipped them in the oil and cheese, inviting me to do the same.

Rear Mezzanine

'The most powerful example I have of writing something down and having it happen was the decision that I made to be an opera singer. That decision came directly as a result of writing.'

Marc explained that he initially went to a theatre conservatory, where he had an awful experience, a 'rotten, terrible time'. He left school for a while and went to New York to live. In New York, he got a job as an usher on Broadway. The stories that the other ushers told him of their own lives were sometimes more compelling than whatever was on the stage. A turning point came when he was asked by his supervisor to substitute for an usher who had died that day.

'I sat in the balcony stuffing programmes with the deceased woman's partner while she told me the story of how once she had met Ezio Pinza when she ushered *South Pacific*. I found her story poignant – her greatest accomplishment a reflection in someone else's glory. She was a bitter person, a bitterness that I think was born out of feeling marginalized.'

Marc started working on a play based on that usher's story; he called it *Rear Mezzanine*. The play was about a young woman and an old woman who, night after night, handed out programmes and showed patrons to their seats in the back of the theatre. The young woman wants to sing opera, but is too afraid to do it. The older woman had wanted to be an opera singer, but had given up and spent the rest of her days in the rear mezzanine of her own life.

'As it turns out, they are both halves of the same person,' Marc says, chuckling. 'That's probably where it got bad. But you have to remember, it was a first play by a twenty-two-year-old writer.' When he wrote the play, Marc knew little about opera, and had no interest in pursuing it as a career himself. He used the opera *Tosca* as a motif only because a friend of his told him that in that opera, Tosca throws herself from a parapet. Perfect, thought Marc; now the older woman can commit suicide in the last act by throwing herself off the rear mezzanine. Marc laughs uproariously at the memory. He had no idea who or what *Tosca* was. His friend played a record for him of the most famous arias and showed him the translation. Marc did not even listen to the opera all the way through.

After a year in New York, Marc went to Colorado College, where he continued working on the play. It won a school competition and for the prize, the play was produced. As he watched his words come alive on the stage before him, he had a revelation.

'I was blissfully unaware of the message of much of what I wrote until I sat in the audience and heard my own words spoken back to me. Here I had written this play all about having the courage to pursue the dream of becoming an opera singer without even realizing I wanted to do it myself.'

Marc found himself asking the same question the play posed.

'The question for me was, Am I going to go on stage, or am I going to stay in the rear mezzanine of life? Am I going to be in the light, in front of everybody, on the stage, or am I going to be – metaphorically – in the background of my own life, watching others perform?'

Marc mentioned Julia Cameron's *The Artist's Way*. Cameron talks about 'shadow artists', people who live in the reflected glory of other artists, not realizing or wanting to face talent of their own.

'I had to ask myself, Am I going to be "in the shadows"?

'It was because I wrote it down, because I saw it acted out, that I knew I wanted to become an opera singer. My career began as a direct result of that play.'

Marc went to the music department of Colorado College to find a voice teacher.

'I approached it with the same enthusiasm I had first greeted theatre. Because I was a tenor and had a strong voice, I immediately got recruited for singing in the music department's lunchtime recitals and performance classes.'

Auditions were held for the Colorado Springs Opera Festival that same month, and Marc became part of the chorus. Three months after his play was produced, he sang his first solo line in an opera; it was three words. 'A humble beginning,' he calls it, but nonetheless a beginning.

And before long, Marc was offered his first major role. He sang the part of Spoletta in *Tosca* for the Opera Colorado in Denver.

He was backstage and heard the soprano singing the very same aria he had used in his play. Suddenly he realized the irony of it.

'I stopped and looked around, and thought, Ahh, here I am, here I am, in *Tosca*. Who would have thought?'

For the next ten years, he never finished an engagement without having booked another one for the future.

for casting the operas at the annual festival held in an outdoor amphitheatre on the grounds of the Puccini estate every summer. To audition in front of him was an honour and a privilege hard to obtain, and here he was in the audience because he was a friend of the school's director.

'When you consider it, it is an extraordinary thing. I was there on a special *Borsa di studio* scholarship for students, not for opera singers. I wasn't there to sing, but to study Italian; in fact, I was the only musician in the programme.'

Writing in Reverse

When Marc wrote his play, he did not realize the longing in his own heart. In some ways, he was working backwards. He had the answer before he knew the question. This 'blind' approach is perfectly in keeping with Laura Day's exercises in an unusual book called *Practical Intuition*. Marc told me of a situation when one of Day's exercises combined with his writing to once again point to a pivotal change in his life. He explains the procedure.

'Laura Day recommends writing down questions, folding them, then placing them randomly in numbered envelopes. Over the course of a few weeks, you "answer" the questions by writing stories, but you don't know which question you are answering, nor do you take the time to analyse the story until after it is written.'

The kind of story-writing Day is suggesting is not a full-blown narrative, but ideas that come to you around any visual image that springs into your mind when you get quiet. In fact, she says to 'allow that image to make up a story about itself'.

Marc was intrigued by this challenge. The picture that

came to his mind was that of a small boy drowning. Here is the 'story' he wrote:

> *A boy drowns in a lake and goes to heaven, which is filled with rainbows and pink clouds and other dead children. Then he returns to the lake where he is saved by a kind old woman who used to be a championship swimmer. Their picture appears in the paper and they become friends for life. Every year she sends him a Christmas card from her home in Rome.*

After writing this story, he picked an envelope and opened it.

The question was, Should I become an Episcopalian, a Catholic, or neither?

Marc was stunned.

'It was an extraordinary affirmation. The fact that the boy was saved, and then the water imagery, heaven, the cards from *Rome* at *Christ*mas, all seemed significant to me. I wrote for ten more pages in my journal, analysing the imagery, asking myself the question, What do these symbols mean to me? It didn't have to make sense to anyone else.

'I called the pastor at St John Fisher the first thing the next morning and told him I wanted to become a Catholic.'

Marc signed up for instruction and the following Easter he was baptized and confirmed in the Catholic faith.

Now he is a cantor at the masses at St John's, and leads the congregation in song every Sunday.

Touching the Divine

Why is it sometimes so hard to formulate a goal, to spell out what we want?

Are we so unsure of our desires, or do we think we are not worthy? Are we afraid of being greedy? Any one of those might apply, but Marc has another, intriguing take on the difficulty.

'Inherently, all of us are afraid of the divine. There is a power in asking for these incredible things. I keep coming back to the term "shadow artist" – all of us, to one degree or another, live in the rear mezzanine of our lives. There is a constant movement towards the light on the stage, the divine light on stage if you will.'

Even as we are drawn to the light, it frightens us and we shy away.

'I see it all the time: people minimizing their dreams.'

INSTEAD of being a 'shadow artist', reach out and touch the divine in your own life.

• NOW YOU •

The subconscious speaks to us in many ways. For Marc, it was through writing a play and seeing it performed. His subconscious created a character who was a mirror of his own longings.

How do you know what you want? How do you know what your own goals are? How can you filter through lots of ideas to know which ones are important?

If you are not even sure what you want, let alone how to get there from here, let your writing help point you to the path you were meant to follow.

1) Early morning writing is a perfect vehicle for crystallizing your desires. Set the clock for a time fifteen minutes before you ordinarily rise and start writing as soon as you wake up. Bring the pad and the pen right into bed with you, write sleepy, twilight-zone thoughts. Write about the irritation in your eyes if your eyes hurt, if you wish you could go back to sleep, write about that; these are 'warm-up', stretching motions before the exercise begins in earnest, because after you run out of things to complain about, your pen moves on and starts giving you some useful direction. Do this faithfully for two weeks without rereading what you wrote and then, at the end of the two weeks, read it over and notice the pattern.

2) Frame three questions about your life, write them down, fold them, and place them randomly in numbered envelopes. Over a period of several days or even weeks, meditate, then look up and write a quick story about whatever catches your eye or comes into your mind. After you have written the story, open one of the envelopes and see what question you have answered. Read Laura Day's *Practical Intuition* for more details on this technique.

Through your writing, your subconscious is letting you know what you want. Writing speaks to us, gives us clues, sometimes in roundabout ways. Listen carefully. Use your writing to interpret the symbols.

And think big. Don't be afraid to touch the divine in your own life.

'Your playing small does not serve the world,' said Nelson Mandela in his inaugural speech. 'Who are you *not* to be great?'

3

GATHERING IDEAS:
A SUGGESTION BOX
FOR THE BRAIN

Once you start writing your goals down, the brain will send you all kinds of new material: innovative, energizing ideas for planning out and expanding those ambitions. That is the good news. Now for the bad: You will forget the best of the plans and ideas if you don't come up with a system for recording and reviewing them.

Flash floods of insights come – and go – quickly.

'The horror of that moment I shall never, *never* forget,' says the king in *Alice in Wonderland*. The queen's quick retort: 'You will though, if you don't make a memorandum of it.'

I recommend that you purchase and carry with you a small memo pad to gather your ideas immediately as they come to you. In many large companies, wall boxes inviting comments foster creative contributions by employees. Similarly, this tiny notebook in your pocket will become a kind of suggestion box for your brain, inviting ideas by the fact that you carry it on your person.

One example of a small memo book that helps get the job done is a wheel book.

'You can't build a house without a wheel book' is the expression my close friend Nancy used when she was constructing a residence in Texas from the ground up.

'Wheel book' is a nautical term. Nancy's husband Eric is a retired navy captain; at one point they lived aboard a forty-one-foot sailing ship. The navy uses a large thread-bound green memo book to chart the activity at the helm (in the wheelhouse) and smaller versions to track jobs to be done around the ship. Every conscientious individual on the ship carries one, from captain to chief to seaman. A wheel book assures accurate accounting.

The first contractor Nancy was working with in Texas constantly promised things on which he did not follow through, frustrating Nancy immensely – until she hit upon the solution: he needed a wheel book to write things down.

When Nancy gave the contractor a wheel book, his performance improved immediately. Since then, the motto 'You can't build a house without a wheel book' has become for me a catch phrase to embody the necessity of capturing on paper the strategies surrounding any big task I am working on. Whenever I have a goal in motion, a dream under construction, I carry a wheel book devoted exclusively to that project. In fact, I often emblazon Nancy's credo across the front of a small book as I christen it for a new adventure. 'You can't build a house without a wheel book' applies to constructing more than new residences.

Although a wheel book keeps track, in one convenient place, of the people to call and jobs to get done, it is infinitely more than that.

Having a place to record your musings and keeping it

and a pen nearby sends a signal to the brain, 'I am ready for your input'.

Carrying a little book with you honours the ideas that come to you, and when you do that, the part of your brain that comes up with these suggestions will be so thrilled to get a little attention and respect that it will send you even more. You will become a hotbed of lively suggestions sparking your imagination continually.

Titbit Journals

A titbit journal is another kind of collection box for ideas. In *Put Your Heart on Paper*, I describe how Sara Rashad used a titbit journal while travelling, as a place to jot down images and phrases she saw and heard during the day. Later, at night, she would transfer those titbits to her larger format journal, expanding the narrative. Sara said that carrying this little book with her was not just for remembering details, but made her pay attention in a sharper way to what was happening all around her. She said it put her 'in tune with every moment'.

When I gave a two-week workshop in Skyros, Greece, to an international audience, I brought with me from the States tiny books, replicas of old-time school composition books with marbleized covers. Across the front of each little book I wrote each student's name and the word 'titbits'.

I told them to take the book wherever they went and jot down concepts as they came to their mind, perhaps images they might want to write up more thoroughly later, or plans to put in motion once they returned to their own countries.

By the second day, they told me warmly that having a

place to record their impressions was keeping all their senses alert. It was helping them notice more, be more aware. It was encouraging them to think.

I still chuckle when I remember how I'd see my students everywhere on the island, making 'titbit' entries – on the beach, at the taverna, at the folk museum. One night we all went dancing at a nightclub on the edge of the Aegean called Skyropoula. There was Briano, a member of the class, in the midst of all the merriment, sitting in a corner with a glass of retsina, as eager as a cub reporter, capturing his fleeting thoughts on paper. What a happy look he had on his face.

By the end of our two-week session together, they knew this wasn't just something to do for a summer course, but for the rest of their lives. They were astonished at how carrying those little books in their pockets had changed their entire experience of being in Greece.

'I found myself,' said Nonnie from Surrey, with delight, 'living twice as much as I did before, because I was paying attention more.'

That's because carrying a titbit journal makes you keener to the workings of the RAS (reticular activating system) we talked about in chapter 1. Having a wheel book or a titbit book ready at hand stimulates your thalamus to alert the cortex: Wake up. Open your eyes. Look and see. Be present to the signs all around you. Life is on your side.

And keeping track of these signs by noting them makes them mount up.

Changing the Conversation

The 'suggestion box for the brain' does not have to be a spiral or a sewn, bound book. It is just as effective – for some, more so – when the 'ahas' you experience are captured and corralled on loose index cards.

During a recent business trip to Manhattan, I had the opportunity to visit with John Sexton, the energetic and charismatic dean of New York University Law School, and my former high school debate coach.

I had read an article about John Sexton in the *New York Times Magazine* that mentioned his peripatetic habit of noting on the go, and was curious to learn more about it. He was happy to tell me about the 'Sextonian suggestion box', which is both portable and potent.

The dean carries a stack of unlined, white, jumbo index cards in his breast pocket. He pulls out one card at a time to make a note as something occurs to him, recording only one comment per card, with the card held vertically.

Once he has written something down in black ink on the white card, he is free to move on to other considerations. It is, as he himself likes to say, 'a done deal'.

He writes on the cards anything that he doesn't want to forget, either personal or professional.

'If I am not thinking about family, I am thinking about school; something will come into my memory bank. Or maybe I'm trolling to see if there is anything that I ought to be doing, or I ought to have done, at home, or to set something up at school.'

Before it escapes him, he jots it down.

The dean says he gets his ideas while walking through

Washington Square Park, or when he's in a car going to an appointment. Sometimes an idea hits him in the middle of the night, or while shaving.

'It might be a thought about a major new direction for the school; something unusual, an inspiration.'

Wherever he is, a card is nearby. He grabs one and writes down the elusive thought.

'Or perhaps an idea is developing and in conversation I'll get a "cut" on it I hadn't thought of before. Sometimes those ideas survive discussions with a colleague and sometimes they don't, so what I will do then is write the idea on a card to make sure it survives.'

Sexton throws out the cards that have to do with appointments or if it's just an information thing; others he gives to the appropriate faculty member or keeps on file until the job is done.

For John Sexton, however, his system of index cards is dramatically more important than a running 'to-do' list, easily dispersed and delegated.

They are integral to his whole style of leadership. The dean has profound philosophical reflections on the part they play in his vision of community leadership at a great university and the whole notion of a leader. He calls it his 'aspirational mode'.

'We have always understood culturally at some level the power of the word and the role of a leader to see things better than they are. Making it concrete actuates it. If you articulate something that is within the community's reach but not yet actuated, the articulation of the goal can move the community towards that actuation. And the same is true of yourself. If you articulate a need, an opportunity, or a concept, you'll start your mind going through the various stages.

'It's not a question of getting the opportunities,' he says with emphasis, 'it's a question of *noticing* that opportunities are there.'

Leadership depends on spelling out for others the oppor- tunities that are there, and on asking the questions. The job of the leader, he says, is to force the community to ask the right questions.

'You are never going to get answers or creativity if you don't ask the questions.'

Sexton is emphatic about this.

'I would put it this way: another way of looking at the cards is that they create an agenda of questions that I am asking. I am not going to get answers unless I am asking the questions, and unless I am putting myself under the burden constantly to want to know why, or how.

'The cards force me to constantly be in a different kind of conversation with the community of people here.'

That conversation is action-oriented, leading him con- tinually to ask the questions that challenge, that push towards the possible.

Collecting Compliments: You Can Bank on It

As anyone knows who has ever had a collection, from bottle caps or football cards to rare coins or stamps, things seem to multiply when you have a place to put them. Before I ever published my first book, I went to the bank and opened an account called 'Bestseller' for depositing book payments. I was nervous about doing that and felt silly at the time –

it had a zero balance for a while. But because I had a place to deposit them, I soon found myself collecting those advances and royalty cheques. Today it gives me great pleasure when I am selling books at a convention and a new fan asks, 'To whom do I make out this cheque?' I grin from ear to ear and say proudly, 'Make it out to the Bestseller Account.'

Compliments are like money in the bank. They both give you a sense of security and they build up a nest egg you can draw upon in times of need.

Designate a container to hold them, a place for them to go and you will watch your deposits grow.

WITH HIS usual good cheer and exuberance, Marc Acito once showed me a tall, faded green antique accounting book he found unused in a secondhand bookshop. He told me he had fired his inner critic and hired a cheering squad instead.

'I decided to write down the names of all the people who have supported me in one way or another. I've got two hundred and ten names here. So far.'

He points to an early entry: *Reaction to Younger than Springtime.*

'I was a freshman at Carnegie-Mellon. The first time I ever sang in front of the class, a woman in the front row sighed. That's on the list of successes. It's a moment, a tiny moment.'

Because he has this book now to record them in, he keeps coming up with names, collecting compliments.

'My ear picks up on them more attentively. Somebody says something nice after a performance; a fan asks for my autograph; I get a flattering letter from a friend; I record it in my Accounting Book.

'I write down what people say about me. I put quote

marks around the words, with their names at the bottom, just to remind me, to give again the boost I got when I first heard it.'

You don't have to be involved in the performing arts to track the kudos and compliments coming your way.

I started one for myself and gave one to each of my children, challenging them to fill the book up with all the nice things people say about them.

As Marc discovered, a Compliment Book can foil the Critic, the inner voice that sows the seeds of doubt and despair. When you falter in your dream, consulting a compliment book reminds you of the character traits that others notice about you. Collectively, compliments are also signs and signals, 'Go! Incidences'. You have more strengths than you might realize you do, until you see them all together and notice the pattern of praise.

Filling in the Blanks

This whole book is about becoming a magnet, a receptor – an adventure about to happen. When you arm yourself with a collection book, the magic seems to happen even more.

That's why it can be a treat to 'fill in the blanks' of a book fashioned along a definite theme. The blanks put you on the lookout for good things happening.

Years ago, I ordered an 'Opera Journal' from the Rizzoli bookstore catalogue. It is a gem of a little book – very elegant, with Victorian pencil art, scrolls and flourishes decorating its three hundred gilt-edged pages. It charmed me no end. Its small clear sleeve, the Lilliputian pages and the interesting separation of sections enchanted me. The first half of the $2^3/_4$- by $4^1/_4$-inch tiny tome is a 'Subject Index', a place to list performances and principals in alphabetical order. The second half is set off by a picture of cherubic angels holding up a sign that says, 'Here the Journal Begins'. This section boasts numbered pages, cross-referenced to the listings in front. A guide in grey type runs across the top of every page in the journal section – reminding you to include the essentials: the name of the 'opera', the 'date' of the performance and the 'place' where you saw it. It was that last column that flummoxed me.

Since moving to Seattle, the only 'place' I ever went to the opera was right here. Indeed, we have a world-class opera company and we do attract the top international voices, but I kept thinking how boring it would be to list only 'Seattle' across the top of every page under 'place'.

Like Sir Edmund Hillary climbing Mt. Everest because it was there, I set my cap to putting some variety in that last column, because it was there.

Soon after, my friend Nancy, at that time living in San Diego, invited me to come for a visit. I told her I wanted to come during the run of *La Traviata*, and she was delighted to buy tickets for herself as well as me.

That performance marked the first 'different' entry in the 'place' column.

A few weeks later, I was asked to give a workshop in New York; the company had two dates available. I checked the Metropolitan Opera schedule before deciding on the second date, which coincided with Rita Hunter singing *Salome*. This was fun. I made up my mind from that point on to arrange my New York engagements whenever possible around opening nights and debuts of my favourite singers.

I extended my plan to other work-related travel. The blank

lines in my little book were the mother of invention. I kept coming up with more and more ideas of how to fill that 'place' column imaginatively. My editor for *Writing on Both Sides of the Brain* lived in Minneapolis; we needed to meet in person for the final, in-depth editing. I scheduled the dates with him to parallel the 'Met in Minneapolis' tour. By day, there were exciting yet intensive meetings with my editor, by night I managed to attend six Metropolitan operas in a row. (Each night I said, 'Opera doesn't get any better than this,' and the next night, it got better.) I like to think the rhythm of the majestic music showed up between the lines in my work.

My greatest coup was when I did a presentation in Cairo, Egypt, and managed to coordinate it around a spectacular *Aida* done outdoors in Luxor, in the desert. The backdrop was the Temple of Queen Hatshepsut in the Valley of the Queens. Now *that* was a 'place' worth recording.

The Opera Journal from Rizzoli had taken on a life of its own and filling in its blanks was changing my life.

I started wondering about the alphabet part of the book; what else could I use it for besides organizing by name titles of operas, artists and composers? I decided it would be nifty to include autographs there.

So I started a campaign to meet the stars backstage and get their signatures. At last count, I had fifty-one autographs, including such luminaries as Plácido Domingo, Jerome Hines, Kiri Te Kanawa, Carol Vaness and living composers such as Alan Hovhaness, Carlisle Floyd and Daniel Catan.

Now I need to order a new Opera Journal; this one is full. Full of fun and full of adventure and travels I never dreamed of when I first sent away for it.

And that's what any or all of these suggestion boxes for

the brain can do for your life, too. Whatever your particular suggestion box is — wheel book, titbit journal or index cards — keeping track on paper changes the conversation in your own head. It helps you to pay attention, to embellish your ideas and record your inspirations. It pushes you towards the possible.

• NOW YOU •

1) Get a small, pocket-size memo book to write in. You don't have to be in a workshop or a new country to capture useful thoughts and notice life happening all around you. Portable pages prompt your brain to give you ways to move your goal along and encourage you to keep track of compliments, 'Go! Incidences', and the signs and signals that you are on the right path.

2) For one week, substitute large index cards for the memo book. Write only one thought, one aha! per card; then note any other ideas surrounding that key one as they occur to you. At the end of the week, ask yourself, How was this different from other systems I've employed? Do I want to keep using it or go back to the other way? Did it add to the number of insights I had? Was it easier to sort and file? Continue with the modus operandi that works best for you. Switch off once in a while.

3) Find or custom-make a fill-in-the-blank book that reflects an interest of yours or one that you would like to develop. The applications are limitless: hobbies, athletic events, investment data. And then

watch what happens as you create ways to make entries. Motivated by an urge to fill in the blank spaces in a wine or cigar book, for example, you might find yourself trying out unusual labels and soon become a connoisseur.

Or try this clever idea from a friend of mine who relocated to a new neighbourhood and was having trouble making friends. She bought an address book and determined to fill it only with new acquaintances. Her book became a vehicle for meeting new people.

Get a book like this for yourself even if you haven't moved; promise to enter only people not in any other address book you already own. Watch how fast it fills – and how rich in friendship your life becomes.

When you have a suggestion box for your brain, you will find yourself living twice as much as you did before.

4

GETTING READY
TO RECEIVE

'There is a difference,' says Napoleon Hill, 'between wishing for a thing and being ready to receive it.'

How do you discern the difference? How do you know when you are ready or, if you are not ready, how do you know what it will take to get to that stage? Gloria's story is an inspiring example of preparing for a goal.

Gloria's Story

'A man stands up in front of me and says, "Would you like to have a drink?"'

She looked at him, and then turned to the friend who was with her.

'Should we?'

Her friend whispered back, 'I have to get home,' so she said, 'Stay for a couple of minutes.'

So he sat down.

'That was it. That's how I met him. I'm convinced that the angels *whooshed* him out of the chair' – she is laughing now – 'because it was time.'

Gloria is describing to me, still with a sense of wonder and delight, the night she met the man who would become her husband.

They started to talk; she liked his sense of humour and the way he dressed. The friend who was in a hurry asked him all the pertinent questions right off.

'So we knew his name was Ted and we knew he was widowed for three years, we knew he had a twelve-year-old child, we knew he was a lawyer; we knew all of this in under ten minutes. Then he and I were sort of flirting and my friend said, "I'm leaving, is that OK?" and I said, "Fine," and she left us there.'

Gloria and I met at a workshop I was giving in New York City.

She and Ted have been married for sixteen years now, yet the recital of their coming together is as fresh as though it happened yesterday. A history like this doesn't go away and never gets old in the telling. It is a tender love story and, as much as anything else, it is a story of preparation and patience – an insight for those who ask, What does it mean to get ready to receive?

They chatted for a while and then he offered her a ride home.

They were riding uptown from Forty-fifth Street and Second Avenue, when Ted turned to her.

'I think you might be the answer to my mother's prayers to Saint Jude.'

'Excuse me. You're *my* mother's prayers to Saint Anthony.'

And that was how they met.

How the Letters Began

For two years, Gloria lived her life out of the conviction that this moment would come – she just didn't know when. Because what is unique about Gloria and Ted's story is that Gloria had been writing almost daily letters to Ted for twenty-two months before they met.

How did the letters begin?

When she was in her late thirties, Gloria found herself one night talking to a married friend of hers about how much she wanted to have a husband herself.

'It was my friend who told me then that when she was ready to have each of her children, she had written letters to a soul, before the children were born, to attract the kind of child she wanted.'

Gloria decided to adapt that idea to her own circumstances. She started to write what she calls her 'soul mate letters'. Those letters precipitated a shift in Gloria's thinking.

'What writing those letters did for me was help me to feel how real it could be. Then I thought, If this is real, then it's just a matter of time. I just had to wait and it would happen.'

From the very first letter, she shares candidly with her unknown companion. She also understands, on an intensely personal level, that readiness to receive entails a willingness to work at it.

Dear Soul Mate,

My soul gets restless thinking that I might be alone in this life. My deeper feelings, when I am clear, help me to see that this is not true, that you are there for me if I feel my

desire for you and am willing to lose my boundaries, willing
to give over to another and not have such a neat existence.

I am ever more in touch with my inner splits that keep
us apart. As I acknowledge them, we come closer to being
together. Do you see me in your heart also?

Let us be together soon.

Amen.

Visualizing Her Desire

To further quote Hill, 'No one is *ready* for a thing until he
believes he can acquire it. The state of mind must be *belief*,
not mere hope or wish.'

Gloria was sure and she used her writing to help underscore that surety by visualizing in writing the qualities she
desired in a partner.

'If you know what you want, you can have it,' says *It
Works!*. Gloria continually wrote out her visualizations of
what would be for her the ideal partner, crystallizing her
own concept of what she wanted in a mate. He would have,
first, '. . . *a love for life*,' and then,

He is not afraid of strength or weakness in a woman. He
admires it and nourishes it.

He will need me. He will need my vision and love of life.
He will be grateful for my hopefulness.

Together there will be nothing we can't do or be. We will
stand together yet separately and will nourish each other.

Gloria repeatedly wrote her picture of what her beloved
would be like, his personality as well as his appearance.

He has dark curly hair, blue eyes, an average build, a trim waist. He understands and is sympathetic to Italian family life. He likes short, red-haired women with good bodies.

It scares her a little to be so specific, so she stops to defend it.

(Soul Mate, I need to be concrete in this visualization, so that I do not shirk my real desire for you.)

Then she continues:

My man will see me clearly and know my needs and wants. I will see him and know, really know, his needs and desires. We will laugh and play together.

The more lucid your list of the 'conditions of satisfaction', the more easily the world can cooperate in giving you what you want.

Soul Mate, I see you again as medium height, strong, nice-looking, with curly hair, light eyes. Strong hands, deep integrity and spiritual truth, a businessman with a sense of security and knowledge about making and having money. Not for its own sake, but for the joy, love, peace and bounty it can bring the world.

She is confident that they will share a deep inner connection as well as enjoy some of the same outside activities.

You will have a high energy level to accomplish tasks and yet be willing to relax and be lazy, to connect with

yourself and me and our marriage together. You will have
my interests in sports, music, dancing, art, spending time
with friends. You will dress beautifully, comfortable in
casual dress or evening wear and want to enjoy life as
I do. Sexuality and sensuality will be embraced by you.

She imagines what life with him would be like:

Every day I experience more clearly what it will be like
being married to you. The sense of well-being and sharing,
the love, the growth together.
   I see us with a warm, loving marriage and mutual respect
and love to help our lives develop.
   How I long to share my life and be with you as your wife.
   May God grant us being together as soon as possible.
   Amen.

Weeding Out What Isn't Working

Ted and Gloria were married in February, eleven months
after they met. It seemed almost too good to be true; yet
Gloria realized she had worked hard to be at this place and
she deserved it.

'In the process of writing it down, of visualizing, there is
a constant surrender, a constant working on the issues that
keep you from your fulfilment. It's not only about writing
things down. There is a parallel course, there is work that
has to be done.'

Gloria was insightful enough to know that events happening (or not happening) outside us are often merely a reflection of our own inner struggle.

Dear Soul Mate,

My task lately has been to get rid of old ghosts. Before I can be free to be with you I need to let go of the past. That is what scares me now. I'm in the abyss. That in-between state of then and now.

The major preparation has been to acknowledge how afraid I am to love you in your physical being. You can see how I create distractions not to be with you.

My soul longs for and fears the intimacy we can have together.

The answer for Gloria was an act of continuous relinquishment.

Dear Soul Mate,

I haven't spoken to you directly for a while. I have been placing my wish in our Father's hands, awaiting their fulfilment.

I continue to work on the inner surrender and trust needed to challenge my 'no' to life and convert it to a 'yes'. I commit to more prayer, meditation and space to allow the inner work to evolve.

She welcomed the challenge and at the same time acknowledged the frustration. There were days when she did not even feel like going out.

I'm in hiding, Soul Mate. Today and yesterday were difficult. It's the feeling that I'll never find you, that God plans for us not to meet — which is absurd since I don't know what God intends. I can only have faith.

But today I felt I could attack any man who passed me. I felt so desperate. When I feel that way I want to lay low and hide. You understand of course that I'm not hiding from you. I do so want you in my life.

This morning and last night I felt so alone and I so wanted your presence. I need holding and sharing. You will bring me these things and I hate waiting for them.

I want you now *but know it does no good to demand.*

About a month before she met Ted, Gloria hit her lowest level of despondency. She met a man who she knew in her heart was not going to be the one, yet she was still disheartened that she did not connect with him.

'I was so discouraged in that moment. How many more men will I have to meet before this is possible? I was ranting and raving, how many more?'

Because of her writing, though, her disillusionment did not last months or even days. It lasted twenty minutes and she went past it.

'It was like a nightmare. It was horrible and I cried and it seemed like I was in the depths of despair, and right behind it was my faith again. I always came back to the place of saying, "This is possible."'

And then she went back once more to writing.

Dear Soul Mate,
  My heart of hearts knows I need solid love, friendship — and patience — as I wait for you.
  Please come home soon.

A Birthday Wish

After writing her letters for a year, Gloria announced her target date on New Year's Eve.

Dear Soul Mate,

This is an important year for us. I expect us to be together by my fortieth birthday. I've asked our Father to grant me this birthday wish. I am nourishing my complete faith that our time has come.

I am ready for you. Demanding doesn't work. Faith will bring us together.

I gently wait for you. I will lead my life, be open, and you will appear before me.

So please come home to me and let's start our life together. Yes, this fortieth year. By my birthday, please.

I love what we will have together, Soul Mate, and look forward to our lives.

Then, a week before her birthday, she dares for the first time to add *husband* to the salutation.

Dear Soul Mate and Husband,

I believe we will be together soon. I've been preparing for your coming now for many years.

And she outright invites him to come to her party, telling him the date, time and place.

I do so want you here for my birthday party next Saturday, April 9, at 8 P.M.

He didn't come.

Apparently, Gloria needed more preparation, more patience. The letters that follow accept that reality, while refusing to interpret his not showing up to mean that he wasn't coming at all, only that it would take longer.

I pray that your preparations to be with me and my preparations to be with you coincide soon. Amen.

Being Whole

In the Chinese philosophy of feng shui, the harmony of our outer surroundings reflects our inner balance. In preparing for meeting Ted, Gloria found herself streamlining the spaces where she worked and lived. She consciously made the decision to live a full life whether she was married or not.

'Now with that, there was always a *desire* to be married, but I had to look at my life and say, If you never married, what would it look like?'

In a significant and empowering move, Gloria decided she did not have to be married to have fine china, so she began collecting Royal Doulton and got place settings as gifts. Then she started hosting holiday dinners in her apartment, rather than always being the guest at family functions.

Far from giving up, it was more a matter of living a quality life.

And as she took each of these validating steps, she shared them with her beloved.

I'm becoming so much of who I am. My love, my need and my desires are all right at the surface. My

humour is improving and you should see my water-
colours — I am living as fully as I can and await
your presence and my new task as wife.

I am becoming the woman you would want me to
be, at least the woman I would want to be for you. I
am learning to live with me so I can live with you.

May we be together soon.

Love to you.

Even as she continued to prepare for her bridegroom, Gloria was aware that there were dividends to herself, as well.

I've told you often that I was preparing myself for
us to be together. I needed to feel my autonomy and
zest for life again before we could be together. I have
learned much in this last year that's been vital to our
coming together. The most important lesson is to know
that if we aren't together for years that I will be just
fine. My survival doesn't depend on us being together
but it will be a bonus and reward in life. A specialness.

Can It Be Different?

Gloria was buying fine china, watercolour painting, declut-tering and decorating. She had a powerful, high-paying job, friends and travel, and she continued to use her writing as a means of discovery and growth. What were the issues in her life that prevented him from making his appearance?

Originally, the thought of disagreements in marriage frightened her. It was worrying to see the marriages around her, the fighting between couples, the passion turned to ennui.

> *Dear Soul Mate and Husband,*
> *My 'no' still clings to bad marriage, unhappiness,*
> *people who divorce, some of my married friends'*
> *constant conflict and discontent, not focusing on posit-*
> *ive role models. Yes, if truth is known, I do not envy*
> *those friends whose marriages are difficult and they*
> *have no desire to change.*

The more she wrote out her fear, the more she realized that, ironically, this dread was keeping her from experiencing the intimacy she desired.

> *What has kept us apart is my fear. My fear that*
> *we will fight, get on each other's nerves, feel crowded*
> *and demanded of, lose our desire for sex together, and*
> *take less of life. But ultimately my fear is of drudgery*
> *and hate in marriage. I hold up those marriages that*
> *seem the most difficult as what I will get.*

She asks her soul mate a heartfelt question:

> *Can it be different for me?*

And tentatively begins to explore the ways in which her approach to relationships already sets her apart:

> *I do give a lot to loving and working on relation-*
> *ships. . . . I do trust my channel to truth and honesty*
> *which many people do not bring to their relationships.*

This is the area on which I can build my hope. My commitment to loving and commitment to truth.

These are the ways I am different from the 'bad' relationships.

Poignantly, a picnic with friends and family opened her eyes. In a deeply felt, touching description, she shares with her beloved the scene and describes its meaning for her.

Today I spent the day with several families with lots of children. It warmed my heart to see people as they really are. Not idealized into perfect children, perfect parents or perfect couples. Just people, my friends, who struggle to love, accept and be in God's world. It is this aspect of acceptance that I want to bring to our marriage.

I long to be with you to start our life together. I've particularly cleared some deep misconceptions in the last weeks.

Especially acknowledging my belief that no marriage can work or be fulfilling.

It is these beliefs that I challenge over and over today.

Visualizing Their Meeting

Gloria continued to visualize in writing what he would look like and even how they would meet.

We can meet as part of my everyday life and we will see each other and know we will be together. God's work will manifest almost immediately. The joy and movement that will follow will reinforce God's abundance.

She pictured herself walking into a room and encountering him for the first time.

Soul Mate,
  You will be sitting, chatting with someone over an exciting new idea. You will recognize me as I will recognize you and our importance in each other's lives. We will talk and instantly start a friendship. We will feel the attraction.
  I will recognize you by your looks, and your eyes. Your eyes will reflect a sparkle, a fun, a humour about life, and a knowing.

Her final picture is so sure and confident it spills over into a litany of affirmation.

  Our married life will blend with each of our family obligations and we will start our life together.
  We will be open to what life will give us and willing to work at loving and living. With this commitment everything will be easy.
  There will be a tentative and then resounding 'yes'. Marriage, family, money – 'yes'. Loving, life tasks – 'yes'. Prayer, meditation, giving – 'yes'. Amen.

Two weeks after writing this last visualization, in her everyday life, Gloria went after work to a pub with a friend who was in a hurry. A dark-haired man of average build was in a corner chatting with business friends. He looked over at Gloria, caught her eye, stood up, walked over and offered to buy her a drink.

The first thing she noticed about him was the sparkle in his eyes.

• NOW YOU •

1) Writing a full-fledged description of what you want is one way of saying you believe that it's attainable and you are ready to receive it. The more precise you can be, the more ready you are. Write a visualization in loving detail – not only depicting your goal, but rehearsing what the particulars of your daily life will be like once this goal is realized.

2) If, like Gloria, your goal is to find a loving partner, follow her lead and write letters to him or her. As her married friend found, you can also write letters to your children, before they are conceived.

   Keep in mind how Gloria put it: 'What writing those letters did for me was help me to feel how *real* it could be.'

3) When things are not happening as fast as you would like, ask, through your writing, What more do I have to learn? What is the lesson here for me? What is the waiting teaching me? Let your pen answer your ponderings.

Gloria's words sum it up: 'Then I thought, If this is real, then it's just a matter of time. I just had to wait, and it would happen.'

5

ADDRESSING
FEARS AND FEELINGS

When you write down your goals, your fears of why they won't work, or even the consequences of what might happen if they *do* work often come crashing in on you. The voices of, 'But what if . . .' and 'What if . . .' make a cacophony of sound inside your head, drowning out your dreams. This chorus of concerns can slow down your plans or sometimes stop them altogether.

My friend Janine's experience taught me a lesson about how to handle such fears and feelings.

Janine and I met through her course, Planning Your Trip to France, which I took the year I went to Paris to celebrate the publication of my first book.

In this travel class, Janine teaches what to pack and not pack, how to get around, and what wines are best to buy. She uses a slide show to illustrate the highlights of the major cities and the countryside, gives travellers an insight into French customs and enough Gallic phrases to get around.

What Janine never mentions in the class is how she got her firsthand knowledge of France to begin with. It is a story that changed her life.

Janine's Story

While in her late twenties, Janine went on a 'If-this is-Tuesday-it-must-be-Belgium'-type tour of Europe. She covered nine countries in eighteen days. It was a whirlwind that whet her appetite to return in earnest for a longer stay and immerse herself in the language and culture of a particular country. Easier said than done. She had close connections with her friends, no savings, house payments. In addition, she knew it would be difficult to find employment if she left the job she had – her hard-to-snag teaching position would not wait for her while she expanded her horizons. Mainly, it would cost more money than she even had to pull it off.

At 2:30 A.M. on a January first, only two-and-a-half hours into the new year, on the front page of a spanking new journal she had received as a Christmas gift, Janine noted that resolutions big and small, *long-term and short-term, observable and fantasy*, were darting through her mind. She listed them *in random order*:

1. *To learn French fluently and enough German to get by*
2. *To make and follow through definitely on plans to live and travel internationally*
3. *To write a will*
4. *To appreciate my friends more*
5. *To learn something about plumbing*
6. *To lose weight and maintain it.*

Perhaps subconsciously aware that she had put protective padding of at least eight throat-clearing, courage-gathering, totally unnecessary words around number two, her scariest ambition, she repeated it, uncovered starkly, centred clearly and unnumbered, at the bottom of the page:

I want to go live in Europe and travel in Europe.

Looking back on it now, she realizes that writing it out like that was the beginning, although she never knew at the time where it would take her.

'I didn't have it well-formed. I just knew I wanted to go back for a long period of time, at least a year.'

The fact that her goal 'to live in Europe, to travel in Europe' was on the first page of her journal helped keep the dream alive. Her eye fell on it every time she sat down to make an entry.

Throughout the months that followed, her journal jottings reflect her steadfastness in the face of ambiguity. Her resolutions page was a beacon she went back to time and again.

Life Is a Decision

Janine shared her journal of that life-changing year with me and gave me permission to quote from it. That was an amazing gift. When I read the journal in toto for the three quarters of a year leading up to her trip, I was reminded, over and over, of an important axiom: Life is a decision. At any point in your life, you can *decide* to act one way in spite of feelings urging you to go in the other direction. When you believe in a dream, you need to risk. You could wind up waiting for ever if you wait until everything looks easy. You could wind up permanently living in what motivational speaker Bob Mowad calls 'that great vacation spot, "Someday Isle"'.

'People do that their whole lives,' says Janine, 'waiting until this – whatever – happens before that – whatever – can take place.'

In her journal following that first entry, she talks about her discouragement. Things did not automatically fall into place just because she wrote it down.

'No. No. Never. Life doesn't work that way. People let frustrations cloud their dreams and they give up too easily. They don't believe their dreams will happen.'

There were many times when an extended trip outside of the country looked impossible. She often thought her goal was grandiose, unattainable – irresponsible, even. When Janine had those moments of feeling discouraged and depressed, she kept on writing. She wrote out how she felt.

I am depressed and tired and worried about the future. I am not sleeping well – the last two nights, I have awakened at 2:30 and stayed awake to 3:30 or so. Ticker tapes of 'woulda-coulda-shoulda' go through my head.

A good weekend but I've been continually uptight and distraught. I don't quite trust myself. I often feel like a large human pinball – spronging off one wall after another in a small room. I feel grouchy, insecure, introverted; my goal's getting fuzzy. Depression hangs on my back like a wet towel.

A Place to Park Her Worries

Her most pressing worry was money. Why leave something secure for the unknown?

I must remind myself often of the meaning of 'leave without pay'. That scares me.

Her journal became a place to park her worries. Writing out her fears spared her 'either/or' thinking. Fears and ambition could coexist.

Interspersed with her declarations of depression and discouragement, sometimes on the same day, she made steps so subtle she did not even see them as consequential. The line, 'live and travel internationally' was the constant, as she bobbed up and down on a sea of emotions.

In spite of her fear and uncertainty, she kept doing little things.

. . . called Western University registration today to see about transferring overseas credits and get the paperwork rolling, just in case.

Highline Community College is offering a refresher course in Italian and French on Monday nights. I called to sign up. Pat, pat, pat on the back.

I bought an Olympus OM1 for my trip!! ($150 for body and lens).

She imposed deadlines on herself and kept to them.

My bottom line for deciding the autumn plan must be June. It would give me two months to organize; also fees for the autumn semester must be in by then.

. . . filled out forms for Avignon study; enrolled in a programme for credit at the Faculté des Lettres.

. . . getting in shape – running; working on paring down 'gotta do's'.

Writing made her feelings speed bumps, not roadblocks. Feelings might slow down her pace, but not stand in her way. Janine knew if she kept on heading in the right direction, she would eventually arrive at her destination.

Writing Keeps It Separate

For Janine, writing down her apprehensions was a way of distancing herself, standing on the outside of her concerns, to become an observer of her own life, a court reporter, noting the facts, not being swayed by them. Left unexpressed, her concerns could have grown and overpowered her resolve. Writing them down became a way to vent and move on. On paper, she could talk herself out of her fears.

This 'stage fright' is part of the process of anything new and difficult.
I will never get anywhere if I don't risk; this is a great test in letting go of fear, being myself and trusting.

The Big Picture

Writing down her fears set another element in motion, one which Janine herself was unaware of. Synchronicity was happening all around her. The world was cooperating. Looking back at her whole journal reveals the pattern. Circumstance conspired from January through September to get her out the door and onto another continent.

One by one, her fears seemed to eliminate themselves.

Saying on paper how she felt and what she was afraid of propelled her to action and propelled the world into action on her behalf.

Yet, her biggest fear was lack of money.

'I had no guarantee of a job, no hope of a job on my return because of the budget crunch and all the layoffs going on, but my desire to go to Europe became over-whelming.'

So she filed her application for a leave of absence.

In response to her formal request, Janine received a phone call from the personnel director. On the day that he called, she was feeling downhearted. Had she jumped the gun and made a foolish choice?

The director said, 'Janine, I want to talk to you about your leave application.'

She was sure he was going to turn her down and terminate her employment. She was astonished when, instead of firing her, he told her that since she wanted to go to France and study language, she qualified for a sabbatical. He told her the district had two or three available.

Janine had never thought about applying for a sabbatical.

'I was a young teacher in my early thirties. I thought,

Nah. Sabbaticals were for teachers who had seniority. I also thought they needed to be more research-based, and this wasn't a research trip; it was an experiential trip. Studying a foreign language is what tipped him.'

The director sent the paperwork and Janine filled it out, and the school district granted her a sabbatical, not a leave. This was a great boon, a magical door opening wide, because it meant Janine would be paid to travel and study abroad.

'Back in those days, my take-home salary was $1,600 a month. I was guaranteed $800 a month for the full year to travel, plus medical (a big plus).'

The catch, which was a relief rather than a restriction, was that she had to agree to teach when she got back. One of the requirements of the sabbatical was a two-year commitment to the classroom on her return.

'Since I had been laid off and rehired for five years in a row, and had no guarantee of a job at all, the promise to teach for two years was just fine with me.'

Bon Voyage

So in September, instead of heading back to the classroom, Janine was aboard Alitalia heading for Milan, and from there on to Paris.

After visiting some friends in Cembra in the Dolomite Mountains, she went to Paris where she connected with a group who were also going to the Faculté des Lettres to study. In Avignon, her sabbatical stipend paid for living with a French woman for several months while she earned forty-five credits. The woman, in her sixties, became like a mother to her.

'I lived in a farmhouse where people in the Resistance had rescued and hidden others during the war. I took courses in medieval French, language, French women writers, French history, French culture, French politics. Most of the classes were in English, but the cooking classes were in French, which was wonderful. I took an aerobics class, which was taught in French, and I was the only American in the class, so my language skills got a workout, too.'

After her studies in Avignon ended, she travelled around Europe and Asia by train and by boat, visiting ten countries.

A Tower of Events

That trip changed Janine's life.

Janine could not have anticipated all the things that took place in her life as a direct result of the trip. Many events of the next fifteen years were because of what she did in that one year, and it hasn't stopped yet.

Janine calls it the Lego effect: A tower of other inter-locking events built upon that single sabbatical.

The first trip overseas seemed impossible until she did it; she has been back almost every year since – partly because her trip changed her teaching. Before, she was a social studies teacher; when she came back from sabbatical, she became a French teacher. Several years in a row, she took kids to France over the spring break. She ended up going back to France ten times – so far – taking friends or students, or going by herself.

The forty-five credits from Avignon applied to her salary steps, so it moved her up a pay grade.

As part of her sabbatical, Janine prepared a slide show and

a lecture for the schools and used that as the basis to develop her travel class.

In addition, Janine was so taken with her studies of France in the fifteenth century, she decided to write a novel based on the life of Joan of Arc and her contemporary, the medieval poet Christine de Pisan. The fabricated parts of the story are interwoven with Christine's actual poetry and true facts about Christine's life, as well as a historically correct depiction of the political intrigue and customs of medieval times. Visiting the sites in person made it easier for Janine to describe them in detail, and get a feel for the power of the places she was writing about.

That book is now part of a trilogy of novels Janine is writing based on French medieval history.

See how one adventure builds on another; how doors open upon more doors to explore what's behind? Janine took a leap of faith when she turned in the application for the leave of absence and look what happened. She not only kept her job, she had it guaranteed for two years and received an increase in salary; she became a French teacher and returned to France ten times. She wrote a historic novel based on her studies and has taught travel classes for over ten years now.

The impact that trip had on her life was well worth overcoming her initial fears.

Why Write Down Fears?

I asked Janine why she thinks writing down her fears about going to Europe made a difference.

Writing down your fears, she explained, takes negativity

and anxiety out of the gut. The only thing it creates there is indigestion. A line in her journal sums up this principle.

Writing is a good way to force my negative emotional reactions into words and not stomach churnings.

What made the difference about writing it down?

'I was discouraged, and if I hadn't written it down, I wouldn't have applied for the leave of absence – and I never would have thought in a million years about a sabbatical. Without writing it down, I wouldn't have had the courage to leave my job.

'Every time I opened that journal, I looked back and there it was, "to live and travel internationally". It was always alive, because it was right there on that page. As I made plans and thought about it, I wrote about the plans in that same journal and if I got discouraged, I would write about that and write through the discouragement.'

Janine would go into the writing feeling negative and come out of the writing remembering that there is a lot of joy in travelling.

'So I wrote about the joy. Just because I didn't have any money and was going to give up my job, that didn't mean that it shouldn't happen.'

A lot of people would consider either one of those two factors enough to stop them. Not Janine. She conquered her fears by writing them down.

The lesson is to let your writing be a 'place to park your worries'.

'If you write down your fears as well as your dreams, you start yourself on a path, and something's going to open up to make that path a little less rocky.'

• NOW YOU •

1) When you wrote down your major goals at the end of chapter 1, did you find fears encroaching on your territory almost immediately? Here's a chance to dispel them. Don't leave them inside your head; write them down.

   Writing separates the dream from the fear; writing about your anxiety makes it an entity existing outside of your goal. Janine's plan to go to Europe and her lack of money could coexist. The desire to study abroad and the worry about losing friends sat side by side. Writing down her worries made them matter-of-fact. The fact on one hand need not negate the dream on the other.

   Write down your fears, and take the churning out of them.

2) Find a magazine picture of someone yelling, maybe at a protest rally or on a picket line, or a mean-looking authority figure – hands on hips, self-righteous, smug, superior. Paste this picture on your 'fears page'.

   Write fast and furiously a litany of laments, the sweeping character judgments, the 'in-your-face' carping, the nagging, mean-spirited put-downs. Use the second person and be pejorative.

   > *You're not good enough.*
   > *You'll never make it.*
   > *It's morally wrong to have too much money.*
   > *Fame is dangerous.*
   > *You are not talented enough.*

> *You'll take a pay cut.*
> *You'll lose prestige.*
> *You'll fail.*

Now find a picture of somebody jubilant, hands in the air, open to life, rejoicing, jumping up and down – a 'yes!' face. Maybe a power fist salute and great glee, a big, just-won-the-Olympics smile. This is your 'Hooray Page'.

One by one, turn each and every statement on the 'fears page' into a first-person, present-tense affirmation.

> *I am the best.*
> *I am successful.*
> *My paycheque is soaring.*
> *I am a sought-after expert, admired by my*
>   *colleagues.*
> *I am fearless. I am focused.*
> *What I offer is special.*
> *I use time wisely and well.*
> *When I get out of balance, I find my way back.*
> *My family and friends take pride in my success.*
> *I am rich and famous.*

Writing down your fears takes away their hold on you; writing out the reverse of your fears (and upping the ante, making the opposite statement not just the fear in reverse, but something even more attractive) empowers and energizes you to start thinking differently, to attract the kind of answers that, rather than keep you tied down, go with a worldview of solutions.

6

GETTING UNSTUCK: WRITING THROUGH TO RESOLUTION

In my hometown of Edmonds when the water sparkles down at Brackett Beach and the Olympic Mountains across the Sound are so crisp they look like white-topped ice-cream sundaes ready to eat we call it 'an Edmonds kind of day'. The kind of day when the water is dotted with sail-boats because everyone wants to take advantage of blue skies, fair winds and a following sea.

My triathlon-level superjock brother had a different idea.

'A perfect day for running!' he announced jubilantly.

He had been promising for some time to take his two non-athletic sisters out and teach us a trotting trick or two. Today was the day.

He put on his Nikes, we put on our Green Flash, and together we headed out the door to pound the pavement. Running alongside us, he started us out at a moderate speed, then built up momentum. Soon he was yelling like a drill instructor whipping a platoon of scruffy recruits into shape.

'See that Volkswagen?' he bellowed, pointing to a red VW some two blocks distant. 'You see that Volkswagen? You *own* that Volkswagen. Go for it. Go for it!'

Puff. Puff. The Volkswagen. Run for the Volkswagen. Totally focused, single-minded, heading for the parked car, we ran and we ran.

Then, as we neared the red Beetle, before we could stop, touch the bumper, and claim completion, he switched land-marks.

'Forget the Volkswagen! See that hill? You *own* that hill. Go for it. Go. Go. Go. Keep on going!'

Puff. Puff. The hill. The hill. Run for the hill.

Once more, the destination changed as soon as we got near it. We continued to run. He continued to target, over and over, ever new, ever further points.

By the end of that morning, we were ready for fratricide, but we had to admit, it *did* in fact get easier as we went along *and* we had never run as far in our lives as we ran that day.

When I am stuck, not knowing what to do next to bring my dreams to reality, I use a technique I call 'Writing Through to Resolution'. My brother's moving markers on that day of running has become a metaphor for me to write and write, covering as much ground as possible – until up pops an answer.

First I put on my mental trainers and write something, anything, to get the pen moving, to set words down on paper, even if what I write is, 'I don't know what to write.' When I get towards the bottom of the first page and start to slow down, I challenge myself to go to the bottom of the next page: You *own* that page, I exhort myself: Cover it. Cover it. Keep on writing.

In Tai Chi, this practice is called 'extending chi', when you train your focus on something beyond your original bull's-eye, or what you thought was the extent of your capabilities. This is how the martial arts master slices through a block of wood with the side of her hand, by concentrating her energies on something beyond the block.

Owning first the VW, then the hill – covering that page, then the next, then the next – lengthens the focal point while it measures your progress. It forces you to go beyond selfimposed limitations, further than you thought possible.

Grumbling OK

In *Writing on Both Sides of the Brain*, I encourage a form of getting ideas out which I call Rapidwriting. It means to write fast without stopping to consider, to edit, to re-arrange or critique. Use Rapidwriting when you cover the page, ploughing through objections, mowing down the inner voice that criticizes your every word. Write whatever is on your mind. Tell the truth. It's OK to burn up your Rapidwriting pages ranting and raving. The Yiddish word for it is 'kvetching', which is complaining raised to an art form. It feels good to get it out. Kvetching is therapeutic.

And the brain has a gift for you in store – a reward for your perseverance. I call it 'Writing Through to Resolution', because when you keep on writing when you would rather stop, the grunting and grumbling peels back the layers, and inevitably turns into a solution and an action plan.

Maybe you feel mad when a goal seems stalled, or you are upset about a situation that seems out of your control. Underneath anger is often fear. Writing through to resolution unmasks the fear and then goes on to answer, What comes next? Where do I go from here?

Nan's story is a good example of writing through to resolution. She took a predicament that looked hopeless and turned it into something positive.

Nan's Story

Nan sings in the church choir with me. We are also taking a course together studying the Hindu Scriptures from the fifth century B.C., the *Bhagavad Gita*. The *Bhagavad Gita* emphasizes the importance of meditation, and Nan said in class one day that writing was a kind of meditation for her, especially when she wrote without stopping, writing down whatever came into her head.

Later, Nan shared with me how writing through to resolution had helped her through a crisis.

Nan works for a brokerage firm. She was distraught when her boss left, and her own job was thrown into question. She knew she was valued as an employee, but it was unclear how his departure would affect the firm – and her job.

'My job depended on him. I did not know who I would be working for, or how I would be compensated. Twenty per cent of my income came from a direct percentage of his commissions, so a large chunk of my salary walked out the door when he did. Would my duties and responsibilities change?'

She was asked to write a job description of her work, including the percentage of time she spent on various tasks, and how she thought she should be compensated. In the business world, this is known as a 'desk audit' and, for some, it is every bit as dreaded as the Inland Revenue variety.

'It was an overwhelming task. I was angry. I had been at that company for ten years. Aren't they supposed to tell me what I do?'

Nan said it was like having to write her own job proposal, for a job she already had. It seemed an insurmountable task, to account for her hours and efforts, to justify what she did.

'I felt like I was going to explode unless I released my anger.'

Her husband, David, said to see it as an opportunity, a chance to express what she thought she had to offer, to know 'how I was an asset'. He told her to sit down and write out her thoughts.

'I wrote for three hours. I wrote and I cried, I wrote and I cried. It was painstaking. I wrote first about the anger and frustration. It was full of venom. I wrote down everything that went through my head – I did not censor it.'

I hate this. I don't want to do it. My heart's not in it. How do I – no – <u>why</u> do I have to convince people that I've worked with and for, for almost ten years, what I can do?

What <u>do</u> I do – I don't know how to quantify it. I hate this. I hate this. I really hate this. It makes me mad. I don't want to do this. I don't know where to start. I haven't had to write a paper in 20+ years. Uck. I hate this. God – I won't be flowery here – please help me figure out what the hell I want to do.

I feel like a child – kicking and screaming the whole way. What is it that makes me good at what I do? <u>Am</u> I good at whatever it is that I do? I never thought I'd be in the brokerage business. What expertise do I have?

*I'm not getting anywhere. What will I write that will be
so revealing? Why don't they all go crawl in a corner? I hate
this. I really hate this.*

After pages and pages of virtual pillow pounding, Nan
begins to unmask the feeling beneath the anger – fear.

'I was scared. I was frozen with fear. It's not that I feared
I would lose my job, but I was afraid that it would be dimin-
ished.'

She felt insignificant and small, her contribution felt
worthless.

'I had a fear of unworthiness, a fear I would be shuffled
into oblivion.'

She did not know who to turn to.

*Who is on my side? I don't trust anyone. That makes
me sad – that makes me afraid. I wonder what they
really think.*

She asks herself what she is most afraid of and comes up
with a catalogue.

*I am afraid I don't know how. I am afraid I'll fail.
I am afraid I'll look foolish and be thought less of. I
am afraid I don't know what I want to do. I am afraid
most of all that after I've figured it out, I won't be able
to deliver.*

Resolution

Once she had spelled out her worst fears like that, Nan
started to calm down.

I must be making progress because I feel less fear and more curiosity than when I began. I remember feeling this way when I had to write the autobiographical statements for college applications.

She numbers her fears and then bolsters her confidence with comebacks to each one.

1. *It's not that I don't know how, I just haven't learned yet.*
2. *'I'll fail.' Well, better to do something badly than to not have tried at all.*
3. *'I'll look foolish – thought less of.' There is always that risk – build up confidence.*
4. *'I don't know what I want to do' – there's an honest statement. Maybe I should just start in the direction where I have the most experience.*
5. *'After I figure it out I won't be able to deliver.' Take it a step at a time to find the holes.*

Once she worked through the anger and the fear, Nan was free now to answer the question, What *do* I do? She kept on writing.

. . . what I bring to the table is worth the cost. I am good at (not perfect) helping other people get what they want accomplished, accomplished. I think I listen fairly well.

Before she knew what was happening, she had filled three pages with her daily, monthly and annual contributions to the company, and moved immediately on to a compensation plan.

'I had to get past the anger, and through the fear. Thoughts were racing through my mind. Since the pen was already in my hand, I started brainstorming the ballpark figures on paper. I was doing what I thought I could not do.'

Right from those raw pages, Nan typed up her compensation package. She gave the proposal to her immediate superiors and the president of the company. They were so satisfied that they matched her previous wages.

'They raised my salary so I was getting at least as much as I had been earning with the commission percentage, and then they gave me a bonus.'

The endorsement from her supervisors was gratifying, but even more satisfying was what 'Writing Through to Resolution' did for Nan personally.

'It was a learning process and a relief; a validating process for me. From absolute hopelessness, I came through the other end filled with hope and promise. It was good for me to define what I do. I am so busy all the time, and then on to the next thing, I don't stand back and look at all I accomplish.'

Because she kept at it, kept on writing even when she wanted to stop, she was rewarded with a new appreciation of her own self-worth and her contribution to the company. She put her pen to paper and did not stop. When it was over, she looked at herself differently. She felt like a new woman.

• NOW YOU •

When you have reached an impasse in your goal, and you don't think you can go any further, pick up your pen and write without stopping. Write through to resolution. If you find yourself angry at a turn of events not going your way, chances are beneath the anger is fear. Let your writing help you come to the fear.

If the situation seems hopeless and you have exhausted all avenues (so you think), if you know where you want to be and don't have a clue how to get there, my best advice to you is: Cover that page and keep on writing. Cover the page, and the next page, too. You *own* that page. Cover it, cover it and while you're at it, go on to the third. You will be surprised at your own power and the solutions you will generate. You will experience a shift in your thinking – a breakthrough.

Beyond the whine, something is waiting. When you go on instead of give in, you get a sudden burst of energy and often a surprise for going the extra mile. Remember those three little words: keep on writing. The best stuff, the aha!, is often right past the place where you think you have run out of ideas or solutions.

Almost seamlessly, before you know it, your complaining will shift to a 'I suppose I could . . .' and then, subtly, to a 'To-do today'.

Push on, keep on writing, until you come to the 'pop'. In the 'pop' will be a plan that will turn what looked like grey skies into 'an Edmonds kind of day'.

7

DOING IT EASY:
LISTING

You need not write volumes to express a goal; a short and simple list of items, as specific as possible, will clarify your intentions as surely as an elaborate description, and perhaps will be even more powerful.

My friend Sydne used listing to make sense out of confusion during a particularly trying time in her life.

Sydne's Story

It had been a rotten year for Sydne; when she found out she had to move, it complicated her life even more. The salvation for her was to use simple listing to define what she could not live without in a new place.

When I went to visit Sydne in her new house, I rounded the corner off the busy street and was startled to see the sweep of the sky circling the houses in the quiet cul-de-sac.

Sydne lived in the middle house, commanding the best part of the view. She opened the door when I knocked and welcomed me warmly. Everything about her home was inviting – the vista of the water, the clean lines of the architecture, the vaulted ceilings. The place had comfort and class written all over it, much like Sydne herself. A perfect match.

Sydne is a registered nurse turned writer, and a seminar leader who presents communication workshops. Her first book, *Code Red*, is an exposé of the medical profession based on her experience of over seventeen years in emergency room and coronary care.

I was pleased to see Sydne looking so relaxed and calm. She put on some tea and brought out a plate of biscuits. I stepped down into the sunken living room with its plush carpet and settled into the love seat.

We sat for just a moment in silence, collecting our thoughts, surrounded by the spacious serenity. The spectacular view of the water seemed to bring its power and placidity right into the living room.

Putting down her tea cup, Sydne said softly, 'I am just coming out of the most harrowing twelve months of my life. I have never been so glad to see a year end.'

The period she spoke of started out well, with the publication of *Code Red*. Her elation at having her first book published was dimmed by her disappointment when the publishing company did not follow through on the promised publicity. Sydne took the promotion into her own hands, setting up book signings, sending out mailings, contacting the media. She hand-addressed 2,500 postcards announcing the book, adding a personal note to each. Her efforts paid off: *Code Red* picked up momentum and began selling well.

Then, Sydne received news that the publishers had filed for bankruptcy under Chapter 11. Because her book was a moneymaker for them, they refused to release her from her contract.

'I was stunned; I had not received any royalty cheques yet and they owed me $18,000. It took me twenty-four hours to recover enough from the blow to clear my head and call a lawyer.'

Ten days after the news about her publisher, Sydne got a shocking phone call. Her aunt called to tell her that her mother had died unexpectedly of a massive stroke. The last time Sydne had seen her mother was six months prior, at the funeral of her grandmother, to whom she was close.

'In less than a year, I had lost both my grandmother and my mother, and then my sister moved far away from me. There was a tremendous void.'

The publishing saga got worse. Within three or four weeks after her mother's death, the publishing company converted their bankruptcy to Chapter 7. Before, with Chapter 11, she might at least get partial payment. Now, she wouldn't get anything. In addition, Sydne had already incurred several thousand dollars in lawyer's fees.

'Not only did I not make a cent off three years of work; it cost me.'

That's when, to compound her problems, her current living arrangement fell apart, and she needed to find a new place to live.

'So I had a horrific year, but now I've been in this new place for three months, with a view of the Sound over-looking Edmonds and the ferry boat, and I am in heaven. The street I am living on is actually called Paradise Lane.'

How did she get from there to here?

First thing Sydne did was to think about what it would look like if she and her teenage daughter were able to have a place of their own, even though it seemed unattainable at the time. She had to stop and consider what was most important to her.

Since she worked at home, she knew it would help her composure and creativity to have a calming view, as far-reaching as that sounded.

For ease and convenience, she wanted the garage to be automatic, so she could push a button and be back in her space.

And she hoped not to have to share a bathroom with her teenager.

Thinking about these criteria helped her define what she wanted. She took a yellow legal pad and wrote down the essentials, what she *had* to have, what she was unwilling to live without.

1. *Two bedrooms; one for my daughter, one for me.*
2. *Two bathrooms, so we don't run into each other.*
3. *A garage with an automatic garage door opener.*
4. *A view of the water.*

She kept thinking. She thought about her mother, a pack rat who collected things; it took a long time to sift through her papers after she died. That taught Sydne a lesson. She likes clean lines and simplicity, and she also believes that 'miracles happen in the space of impeccability'. She thought about the chaos her life was in. She went back to her list and added,

5. *Someplace quiet; beautiful and pristine.*

Sydne kept that list in front of her and looked at it whenever she got discouraged, whenever she wondered if she would ever have a place of her own.

The money she needed soon became available. Five months after her mum died, she received an inheritance from her mother's estate. Now was the chance to make her list a reality and find a new place to live.

With cash in hand, she bought the Sunday paper on Saturday night and checked the classifieds. There were four ads that looked promising.

'Of those four, I crossed off two immediately, after calling and finding out they did not have a view. Sunday morning, I got a call back on the third choice; they had a view of the mountains, a great view of Mt. Baker, but I wanted a water view.'

The fourth ad was short and simple,

2 bdrm 2 bths garage prtl view of Puget Sound.

'I called and made an appointment with the owner. Before I went, I meditated for about twenty minutes, just on nothing. When the mediation was over, I said a quick prayer, 'God, let *something* in my life be easy. I need something easy this year!'

It was love at first sight.

'I met the landlady, I walked in, and that was it. As soon as I came into the living room and saw the cathedral ceiling, the off-white carpet, the view and the deck, I knew. I did not even see the bedrooms and I knew.'

As soon as Sydne got home, she left a message on the owner's answering machine: 'Call me, I want it.'

Not too surprisingly, the owner had some initial

reservations because Sydne didn't have a conventional paying job, with a regular salary. How did Sydne convince her not to worry? She offered her two months' payment up front, authorized a credit check and gave her a powerful reference, the lawyer who helped her when the publishing company went bankrupt.

In spite of the fact that several people were also interested, the landlady chose Sydne as her tenant.

Why Listing Works

Today Sydne rereads her list of five characteristics and looks around herself in disbelief. She got everything on her list – and then some. There is a smile in her voice, then a laugh out loud as she exalts, 'I wrote it down! That's really how I did it!'

Sydne is convinced that writing that list made all the difference.

'Writing a list gets it out of your head. Heads can be dark swamps; the conversations, the constant chatter, whatever you want to call it, keep interfering.

'Writing a list gets it out of the swamp, onto paper. You can see a list in black and white and it's real.'

When you reduce your goals to a list, it helps keep your focus. This is a truism Sydne learned indirectly from giving seminars.

'Every time I get up in front of a room, I have a single intention for the session of the seminar; a three-hour session is formed from one sentence: the intention.'

Keeping that sentence uppermost in her mind guides her in knowing what to say.

In addition, writing a list is a way of clearing your head. According to Sydne, the process of narrowing goals to a list is a matter of sifting through cultural, religious and social conventions to get at what *you* want, not what others want for you.

'When you are vague and general, you are safe. Get to the essence of it; that's when things happen. Nothing can happen when you're generalized and safe – nothing changes.'

Throughout the tough times, looking at that list reminded her that something better was waiting, gave her something specific and definite to believe in. Now Sydne says she has a new motto: Do it easy.

Before she sits down to pay bills, or to work on her new book, when she's picking up the phone to make an important phone call, she first takes a breath and says to herself, 'Do it easy'.

'I've got those three words written down in a couple of different places, "Do it easy" – all of it.'

I walked back to my car thinking of Sydne's new motto, trying it on for size in my own life. Behind me, a smiling Sydne waved good-bye from the doorway of her new house on Paradise Lane.

• NOW YOU •

Use listing as an opportunity to crystallize your intent – to learn what matters most to you.

Keep that list handy, and look at it regularly, especially if you lose heart or feel scared. Emblazon it in your mind. Repeat to yourself: This is what I want and it is waiting for me.

Think of it as a shopping list. Don't be vague and general; be specific. Don't simply write 'car'. Specify the type of car with make, model and mileage. If it's money you want, not just 'money,' but definite sums. Pretend you are sending someone else to the shops, so you want to spell it out, to make sure they come back with the right size and brand.

State it simply. Do it easy.

8

FOCUSING ON
THE OUTCOME

Life is like a labyrinth and the path to successful completion of your goal may be filled with blind alleys and dead ends. How do you keep from losing heart? By focusing on the desired outcome.

I sometimes cheat a little when I am doing a maze puzzle: I do it backwards. Starting from the exit, I work my way back to the entrance point. For some reason, it's easier that way. You can use this same approach in getting your goals. Start from the destination and then figure out how to get there.

A plane flying from the mainland of the USA to Hawaii is, 90 per cent of the time, off course – but it is constantly correcting. The pilot knows he's headed to Hawaii so when the plane deviates, or the winds throw him off course, he checks his needle and magnetic heading, adjusts and gets back on track. Eventually, the plane lands on that tiny island in a huge ocean – on exactly the right, narrow airstrip. So too with goals, we need to check our compass and remember where we are heading.

'Hold It in Your Mind that You Want a Pool'

My friend Erich Parce told me this story once when I was discouraged. His friend, Lou Tice, a well-known motivational speaker, told how his children wanted a swimming pool in their back garden. It wasn't in the family budget, but Lou was never one to discourage dreams. He didn't tell them the pool was out of the question, he just kept answering, when they brought it up, 'Hold it in your mind that you want a pool.'

One day they were all out taking a ride in the car and they spotted a huge pool above the ground in someone's yard – just the kind of pool they were looking for.

'Dad,' they begged, 'let's stop and ask them where they got it and how much it cost.'

Lou was reluctant to knock on a stranger's door, but his kids were so excited, he relented. Can you imagine his shock at the homeowner's response?

'We're trying to get rid of that pool – we hardly ever use it and we want to plant a garden there – would you like it?'

Free of charge, the Tice family now had their pool.

The pool story reminds me of the importance of faith. We need to have faith that we will reach our goals; to bolster faith when it flags, write it down as a reality.

I was invited to give a workshop in Greece but, as the date neared, it looked as though it would be cancelled because not enough people had signed up. That's when Erich told me Lou Tice's story and reminded me: 'Hold it in your mind that you want a pool.' The pool was Greece and the best way to hold it in my mind was by writing about it.

I vowed to write about Greece every single day until I got a call saying that the workshop was on.

> *This summer I plan to be in Greece giving a dynamite workshop to a packed class meeting daily at the Skyros Centre on the island of Skyros. I envision people signing up in droves. A real hoot would be if the class filled up so fast that they were turning people away.*

Using the scenes in the catalogue as reference, I could picture exactly what it would look like to be there.

> *I stop a moment to picture the sunny classroom where I am teaching; I am in front of a group of twenty people writing their hearts out, energized and uplifted. I crawl into bed at night feeling satisfied, and wake up refreshed and energized to the sound of roosters and donkeys, ready to enjoy fresh melon and yoghurt, a morning swim in the Aegean and yoga on the beach.*

Still no word from the sponsors of the workshop. I made phone calls, distributed fliers, sent an invitation to register out through the Internet. Nothing panned out. I was getting discouraged, losing faith. Every time I faltered, I remembered Erich's expression, 'Hold it in your mind that you want a pool' and I kept on writing. I countered any daunting reservations I had with positive emotions.

> *I am getting scared with a little flip-flop in my stomach whenever I think of Greece and pulling it off, but I am*

clear in my intent: to be in Greece this summer, teaching, helping people to feel powerful about their writing and at peace in their souls.

I feel a joy surrounding me, a white light spreading out to the participants, as white as the stucco houses shining in the sun against the deep blue sky against the blue, blue waters of the Aegean. It is a whole and satisfying feeling and, even more, an exuberant feeling, a feeling of jubilance and celebration.

In almost every case, if I kept writing, the discouragement would turn to an action plan or a new visualization. I would follow through on the action – and keep on writing.

For forty-six days I wrote every day, holding that pool in my mind, and then the phone rang very early one morning, with a go-ahead for Greece. The workshop had filled up with people from all over the world.

I look back now with incredulity to see how I anticipated in my writing so accurately exactly what it would be like.

Moving Beyond the Outcome

Emphasizing the ending is one thing, but there is a deeper level you can go to, which will steel your resolve further. I call this deeper level the 'benefit of the benefit' or the 'outcome of the outcome'. Instead of just writing about your target, consider why you want that goal in the first place, how attaining it will enrich your own life or others' lives. To get to this level and beyond, to the levels buried beneath (the outcome of the outcome of the outcome), add to your goal description as you write, '. . . and because of that . . .' and then, '. . . and because of that . . .'

Maria works at a coffee shop called Diva's. She is looking for an apartment 'high in the sky' where they allow pets. She wants hardwood floors and lots of windows, and wants it located near a park.

Early one Saturday morning, we are alone in the shop and Maria eagerly shares with me a description she wrote, on a page ripped from a notebook, of her ideal apartment. When I read her wonderful list, I know she will soon have her dream place, because in every instance she wrote not only what she wanted, but why she wanted it.

> *High in the sky — I want the top floor.*
> *Pets are allowed, for they bring joy!*
> *Hardwood floors, easy to care for.*
> *Near a good park, to run in.*
> *Surrounded by windows for extra light.*

I am not at all surprised when, two weeks later, Maria comes into Diva's with eyes shining — she found the perfect penthouse apartment with hardwood floors and big windows right near Green Lake, and they let her keep her cat.

Sometimes the 'outcome of the outcome' is not as clear and apparent as it was for Maria — you need to let your writing uncover why this goal is so important to you. This is the lesson I learned when I applied for the chance to appear in an opera.

I am a great fan of the opera, so I was elated when I heard that the Seattle Opera was looking for 'supernumeraries', that is, non-singing bit actors, for their production of Puccini's *Turandot*.

I got it into my head that I wanted to be one of those 'extras'.

Alas, when I went down to the Seattle Opera studio to

be measured for the silent part of Lady Pang, I was the wrong size. Even though I told them I would gladly gain pounds or lose pounds, they said it was actually a matter of height. I was too tall. They were very sorry, but first, they had a costume ready for that part that did not fit me, and secondly, the tenor they were pairing me with was short.

So they turned me away.

A chance to appear on stage in an opera was an opportunity too choice to walk away from. I decided that I was going to get that part.

So I went home and wrote about being in the opera.

> *It is so wonderful to be in* Turandot *and I am so happy.*
> *Even as I write that my heart surges — I feel my chest expand and exhale. I am blissful to be surrounded by music that I love, and a part of something so majestic.*
> *I am welcomed and belonging, and the singers smile as they pass me backstage.*

I mentioned to a close friend how near and yet how far I felt to getting this part. She didn't help much by telling me how many missed opportunities she had when she was working as a model and commercial actor.

'That's the way it goes in theatre,' she said.

That was not what I needed to hear. I tried not to dwell on falling into that 'close-call' category.

Writing in the present tense, as though it were already a given, helped to keep the faith, as weird as it felt at the time to do it.

> *I love wearing a costume and all the little touches — like the curl of the toes on the silk shoes — a dresser to help me get*

ready and keep all the parts together — a make-up artist — to fuss over me — the wigmaker adjusting my chignoned hair — all the while my head filled with the magic of it — the shared cama-raderie with the others — the sense of belonging, of teamwork, of pulling together.

At one point, I made the mistake of calling Paula, the production supervisor, to see if they had found anyone else yet and she told me there were three other women coming in that afternoon to be measured.

I am feeling upset. Now Paula says it is not only the height they are concerned with, but they want under 28 inches for the waist. And there are three other candidates. Drat! and double drat!! I want that part so bad I can taste it.

To combat my discouragement, I went back to writing, and this time I went to the deeper level, the 'benefit of the benefit', the 'outcome of the outcome'.

Uncovering the 'Why' Beneath the 'What'

Why did I want this part so badly? What could happen because of it? As I wrote out the answer to those questions, I began to understand why it meant so much to me. Being in that production would help my writing: by colouring my world, by surrounding me with beautiful sounds. Watching from behind the scenes how such a great work came together would help my editing and sense of choices. In addition, this particular opera had a special, personal connection which gave me a jolt of joy just to think about — *Turandot* was the opera I had seen in New York at the Met during the launch of my first book, and I write about the magic of it in my second. I wanted that energy and enchantment to transfer over now to my current project. When I realized that, getting that part took on even greater import and metaphor for me; it became a symbol of what was possible for my third book.

I wrote about the 'outcome of the outcome' in the present tense.

> *Picture this. I am under contract with a major publishing house turning and burning every day at Vivace's writing my little brains out . . . What a joy to be doing what I love, working hard on the editing and shaping of these interviews. It feels so productive, so right . . . creativity soars!*
>
> *Part of what infuses my spirit in this continual high is the fact that many evenings and an occasional afternoon is spent on the boards of the Seattle Opera House rehearsing for Turandot.*

> *. . . As soon as I get on stage or near it, even sitting in the auditorium, my heart goes up a notch, and watching the production come together in bits and pieces informs my writing and my work.*
>
> *. . . what a thrill to go through the 'Stage Door/Authorized Personnel Only' to find myself sharing rehearsals with people I admire, as the stage director's voice over the house intercom calls to me, and the music of Puccini swirls around me. The rhythm is reflected in my writing.*

Two days after writing about the 'outcome of the outcome', I got a phone call from the opera: the person who was supposed to take the part couldn't do it, and they needed me to jump in.

And yes, immersion in the music and being part of such a grand production did help my writing to flow and enhanced my editing skills – and a bonus is, I got to tell the story here.

• NOW YOU •

Writing about the outcome helps you to stay focused, even when you're not focused – or think you're not. The written word keeps the image steady, unwavering, like a lighthouse beam, steady on. It keeps the goal, the intended consequence, in mind. The page can hold it for you.

When you focus on the outcome, write in the present tense, as though you were describing something that is already happening. I call it 'writing as reality'. Be sure to date your description, because when you read it back later, you will have an eerie sense that you wrote it *after* it took place, rather than before, it will ring that true to what transpired.

Now dig deeper. Not just the outcome, but the 'outcome of the outcome'. Don't just write about *what* you want, but include *why* you want it. Why does it make a difference whether you have this or not? And then keep going deeper – why do you want that? And then deeper still, the outcome of that second outcome and so forth, until you hit the core of it.

One way to do this is, as you write, to repetitively fill in the blank, '. . . and because of that I will . . . '

Focusing on the outcome and the outcome of the

outcome keeps your dream alive. The more you concen-
trate on the *effects* your goal will have, in your life and
in the world, the more dedicated you can be in your
mission to achieve it.

9

CHANGING YOUR ENVIRONMENT: GET NEAR WATER TO WRITE

Most of us think writing means sitting at a desk or table with a straight-backed chair, feet firmly planted on the floor, pen held correctly, and paper tilted at just the proper angle. We probably get ideas like this because we associate writing with being in school. But when you are describing your goals, depicting in detail a picture of your perfect plans in execution, or writing through to resolution, it is a fact that creativity often flows more readily when you are outdoors – especially if you are near water.

The connection between water and creativity can be documented back at least as far as the third century B.C. Archimedes the mathematician, tired of wrestling with a problem, went to the public baths. There he submerged himself in the warm waters, luxuriating in the calming sensation. He noted abstractly that as he sank, the level of the water rose slightly around him. Suddenly, aha!, he had the solution to his scientific inquiry.

He had figured out how to measure density through displacement, discovering a method of determining the purity of the gold in King Hiero's crown.

Archimedes was so pleased with himself at the revelation, he jumped immediately from the tubs and, they say, ran through the streets of ancient Athens, stark naked, shouting, 'Eureka!'; that is, 'I have found it!'

By sinking in the water, Archimedes experienced the physical phenomenon that answered his conundrum; but perhaps it was also the fact that he was relaxing his mind by being surrounded by soothing water that led to his breakthrough.

Being near water – one of the four elements of life – is conducive to creativity. Princeton scholar Julian Jaynes says the greatest scientific and mathematical discoveries happen in the 'Three Bs: the bed, the bath and the bus.' The middle 'b' is not just 'bath' but includes all contact with water, including taking a shower, being on a boat, swimming in a lake and walking in the rain.

In Seattle, we are blessed with gentle rains. Plentiful and peaceful falling water: good rain for thinking and for writing down your thoughts. (I carry a waterproof pen and 'Rite in the Rain' paper, a non-porous pad used by surveyors.)

Furthermore, we are favoured with a ferry system that travels back and forth across Puget Sound and plies the waters of the San Juan Islands. Like Edna St Vincent Millay, who was very tired, very merry and went back and forth all night on the [Staten Island] ferry, I have been known to ride for hours, content in the creative solitude this tranquil transport offers me.

Several times I have brought one of my children on the ferry with me, particularly when he or she is working on a project or studying for something big. When Peter was preparing for an important exam, we boarded after dinner, at six, and didn't disembark until ten, with a feeling of satisfaction and giant smiles on our faces, four solid hours of accomplishment under our respective belts. Of course, the element of no distractions, as well as the rhythmic repetition, aided our productivity. And something more – being near water.

Being near water, especially moving water, gets ideas to flow. The particular penchant of moving water to generate creative thought was brought home to me when I mentioned to a workshop group at a holistic centre in Boston how people often get inspired in the shower. I told them half-humorously that since enlightenment can hit you there, it is wise to be prepared with an underwater pen and paper impervious to wetness, or washable crayons to write on the walls.

A curly-haired woman in the front row nodded vigorously as I recounted this phenomenon.

'It's the negative ions in the water,' she contributed cheerfully.

This was news to me, so I decided to do some research on it. I was fascinated by what I found. Studies show that people can react with headaches and fatigue when the air is charged with too many positive ions, due to such things as modern air-conditioning, television transmitters and seasonal winds. To counteract this, so-called 'negative air ionizers' generate an abundance of electrons in the air, making people more energetic and creative.

I passed on this idea of showers and negative ions to an academic group I was addressing in Calgary. A burly Canadian professor approached me at the break.

'I know exactly what you mean. My wife is like that,' he said stoutly.

'Excuse me?'

'I say, "My wife is like that." '

'Your wife is like that? I don't understand.'

'Yeah, so negative in the morning, until she has her shower.'

I did not have the heart to tell him about modern pollution, molecular stability and artificial ionizers. And maybe he hit upon something after all. As Archimedes discovered, water cleanses and water soothes, and water restores our own balance. The very sound or even the sight of water falling nearby can calm us down and bring imagination alive.

A Cosmic Sense of Humour

When I want to spark my own creativity, I seek out places where I feel comfortable writing, where my ideas flow (and I like a good coffee). I have been writing at Espresso Vivace Roasteria, on Capitol Hill, for years, enjoying the energy, the friendliness of the staff – and the best brew in Seattle. One day, with a start, I registered an additional, stimulating feature of my environment there. Even though it was obvious, I had sat there for ages without realizing it. Vivace's is housed in an old school building, looking out onto a reservoir, with a tall shooting fountain in the middle of the man-made pond. When I take my seat at a tall counter window, I am surrounded by water, and when I take a break, I often walk around the track that circles the fountain. Here I was, drinking in the negative ions all around me, without even consciously recording that I was doing that.

It's nice to know that even when I am not watching out

for myself, someone is taking care of me, often with a cosmic sense of humour. One afternoon, I spent three-and-a-half hours writing at the funky Uptown Espresso in the Queen Anne area near the Opera House. I was plugging away so diligently that it was not until the second hour that I looked up and saw something that made me smile broadly, shake my head and laugh out loud. Of all the tables at which I might have chosen to work, I had unwittingly positioned myself and my laptop at the one with a revolving heat lamp that mimicked the perpetual falls of Niagara.

Unbeknownst to me, the moving picture of tumultuous falls had been in continuous motion beside me as I wrote.

Creating an Environment for Creativity

Whatever the rationale behind getting near water, it works. Here are some examples of the principle in practice.

A friend of mine had a shower stall built into his office. At first, he claimed it was for nights when he was running late and had a dinner meeting in town. Finally, sheepishly, he admitted the true reason he installed it. For him, it is like a think tank. A place he can go, even in the middle of the day, to work things through, to think things out.

A workshop participant who is a diver once told me that he got so many good ideas in the shower that he hung an underwater clipboard in there to record them. You can get one yourself at a dive shop for under ten pounds.

Another fellow startled me in class when he reached into his backpack and pulled out a *pocket* negative-ion generator that plugs into the cigarette lighter in his car, to help him think more creatively when he is driving.

And a reporter for *The Seattle Times* told me that whenever she is stumped, with a deadline looming, to get the creative juices going, she gets up from her desk and takes a jog around downtown Green Lake – bringing her pad and pencil with her.

Any of these are practices you can adapt and incorporate into your own life and work situation. To paraphrase Wordsworth's injunction to Michael to get outside,

> *One impulse from a bubbling brook*
> *May teach you more of man*
> *Of moral evil and of good,*
> *Than sitting indoors can.*

• NOW YOU •

Streams, showers and waterfalls stimulate creativity. To create aha! moments in your life, to capture and expand your insights, for inspiration about the shape of your dreams, get near water, especially moving water – and bring a pen and paper. 'Eureka!' you will soon be shouting.

I suggest you put on your clothes before running through the streets with news of your discovery.

10

SCRIPTING YOUR DAILY LIFE

A diary runs your life by tracking your appointments, expense accounts, scheduled events, and whatever else you want to include on a calendar that you carry with you. That takes care of your mundane busywork; how about the spiritual side? Is there a type of daily planner that not only reminds you where you need to show up at a certain hour, but also challenges you to become a better person – in short, not just a to-do list, but a to-be one?

A performance artist named Ron has just such a system. His is a different, fairly unusual way of using writing to direct his goals and his daily life.

Ron's Story

Ron and I met at the 'Three-Day Novel Writing Contest', so you might say we ran a marathon together, a literary tour de force. For three intense days over a Bank Holiday weekend, we sat at adjacent tables at Vivace's and wrote for fifteen to sixteen hours a day, with hardly a word exchanged between us until it was over.

Ron is a young man of many talents and perfect carriage. It was not surprising to learn later that one of his avenues of creative expression is dance. At the time we first met, he was a student of acting and screenwriting, in the middle of rehearsal for a lead in *A Chorus Line*, while converting a novel he wrote into a screenplay.

He is an Adonis of compact energy. In speaking to him, you sense the subdued power beneath the skin. If danger arose anywhere in the world in the middle of your conversation, he might excuse himself politely and with a wry, 'somebody's-got-to-do-it' smile, jump into the nearest phone booth, and emerge as the man of steel, or maybe cross his arms over his chest and morph into a Power Ranger.

Currently Ron is in Texas taking a heavy load of twenty-one graduate credits at Texas Women's University. How does he stay so focused and how does he manage gracefully to cover so much ground in a day? Ron says he does it through his daily 'List of Intentions'.

Putting the Day's Intent in Writing

'I start out every day writing a catalogue of reminders to myself, prompts of how I want to approach my life that day.

'It's a way of connecting to elements which offer significant value in my life. The more I build an awareness of them, the more they will enrich my life. That's why I write them out every day.'

The first thing on his list is,

I monitor and observe my thoughts, directing them whenever possible.

'That sentiment helps me keep in the present. Life is lived in the present. When I am lost in thought, I have separated myself from the here and now.'

The second morning injunction underlines that wisdom.

I focus to be here and now through breathing and sensory awareness.

Ron writes his list as quickly as possible, attempting to come up with all of them from memory. After the first two, they're not necessarily written in the same order each day: however, he disciplines himself not to go back and look at the entries from the day before unless he can't come up with the last few.

'The things I list are reminders to myself of tools, principles and practices that I want to attune myself to in my daily life. Before, I did these reminders as commands, for example, "Monitor and observe your thoughts". When I changed them to present tense and first person, they were more direct.'

I talk less and listen more now, allowing my actions to speak louder than words.

I treat every person I meet as the most important person in the world.

I feel the power of the universe flowing through me now.
People love to give me love and money.
Every dollar I spend enriches the universe and returns
to me multiplied.

Writing out his intent of the principles he wants to guide him throughout his day helps him behave that way, because he is clear in his intent and can correct his course if necessary.

Collecting Aphorisms

Generally, the maxims and affirmations Ron writes come from his extensive reading, or he composes them to tie in with some new skill he is learning to develop.

Or he uncovers by chance an expression that resonates for him. For example, one time he heard the philosopher Jean Houston on a radio interview speak of 'polychromatic time' and thought it was a valuable idea.

'Polychromatic time' means that time seems to pass differently, based on what you are doing and how involved you are.

When you are working at something without any distraction, totally focused, hours may pass and it seems like a few minutes. You live in eternity and in a moment, simultaneously.

So now one of the things he writes to himself every morning is:

I live in polychromatic time, accelerating the richness
of my living.

Several items on the 'List of Intentions' reflect changing needs in Ron's everyday life; they are maxims to help him stay healthy.

I minimize my food portion intake now, eating ¹/₃ to ¹/₂ less food per meal.

When he is in a production, he burns off a lot of calories with strenuous rehearsals. Otherwise he needs to remember not to eat as much.

Another dictum on the list is an incentive to heighten his intellectual and artistic pursuits.

I develop a magnificent obsession, knowing that a drop here, a drop there, soon becomes a flood.

Ron explains that this particular contribution to his list comes from a friend of his who is at the University of Delaware working on an art degree. His painting teacher used that expression to encourage his students to be passionate and willing to work steadily.

Ron's current 'magnificent obsession' is music.

'I want to compose original music even though I do not have a lot of time to devote to it right now. I have been working on music theory, voice, singing and piano. I do the music theory in the bathroom when I get up, using the kind of book where you cover the right side of the page and put the answers on the left.'

Bit by bit, it is coming together.

'I have already finished the first-year music theory book and I am going into the second-year book.'

'Combopop' is a phrase Ron uses to describe deliberately doing multiple tasks.

I do one task at a time to completion, unless I have planned ahead to combopop activities.

'Bruce Lee could be reading a book, watching TV and doing martial arts all at the same time. Each thing took a different part of his attention and so he could do three or four things at the same time and do them with integrity to every item. That's what I mean by "combopop" activities.'

Ron is the first to admit he does not 'combopop' with the intensity of Bruce Lee; but he will, for example, stretch his legs or hamstrings while talking on the phone. If he has not deliberately chosen to do multiple tasks, he concentrates on one job at a time until it is finished.

Another sentence in his daily list reflects an underlying philosophy and creed of his.

I relax above all fear, living from my spiritual self that knows no fear and knows that the universe provides everything for me now.

'Saying "the universe provides",' Ron says, 'is a way of encompassing many beliefs. When I say, "the universe" I don't mean extraterrestrial forces. I mean what Maltz talks about in *Psychocybernetics* – I feed this stuff into my gracious unconscious mind, and the things that I request or the things that I desire begin to appear in my life. People think it's coincidence. But to assume that it is coincidence doesn't give me any influence over it. To consider that circumstances and coincidence can rule my life is to take out any intention on my part. It credits the fates: I'm a frail craft on the sea of fate, to be washed wherever the currents carry me. A lot of people do believe they're fated, and that things are fated in life.

'I don't happen to be one of those people.'

Ron believes it is a matter of being open to things, and letting people know what you are looking to gain.

'Having the intention and being aware of what you are looking for is significant. Once you are clear about what you want, it seems to me, the universe provides: You attract what you need to you. That's one reason I do the lists and affirmations every morning. It's not coincidence.

'If you have a desired outcome, you can influence the probabilities. Just like a Peking opera person spinning plates, you can spin the probabilities to increase the chances of a desired outcome becoming an actuality.'

Go Out Into the Flow of Life

A curious adage on his list raises questions. It turns out to be central to his modus operandi.

I empty my basket of preferences.

The 'basket of preferences' are things he plans to get done that day. By emptying it, he means he is conscious of his calendar, but not bound by it.

'I go out into the flow of life, allowing new developments to occur. As they do, I respond.'

The expression is not original to Ron.

'The lineage of the term goes back to a man I studied martial arts from, who had studied with Bruce Lee.'

You start out the day noting what you want to get done

that day. But don't fill your 'basket of preferences' too full. You might find yourself doing something that is not on your list. If you schedule your whole day, you are not going to have time to do those spontaneous things.

'When a new development arises that has significant value for me, something that outweighs the value of what I had intended, I will do the new thing. So I go out without being locked into any preferences and just be with the world and the universe and respond without any expectations of rewards from other people or from situations. Otherwise, I may be limiting what those situations or people might offer me. If I come in with a preconceived agenda, it's a block. There might be much more I could learn if I was open to whatever possibilities exist, or could come out of the interaction.'

Ron insists that there is a huge distinction between his basket and a time management list. One of the differences is that at the end of the day he is not beating on himself for what he hasn't done.

'There's no reason to be guilty, because then I'm violating the very first thing on my list of intentions: *monitor my thoughts*, and the second, *be in the here and now*. Guilt is in the past.

'I want to do everything I can to spend my time and awareness in the here and now because that's where life is. The bigger I can make the present moment, the richer my life is going to be.

'I stay open for new developments and opportunities, improvising within a structure of intent.'

Dropping Items from the List of Intentions

The purpose of writing out the reminders is to implant them in his mind. Ron has been writing his list for several years now. Ideally, he wants to get to a point where he doesn't need to write them out every day, where they have become automatic axioms that flash in his mind in certain stressful situations. The list changes as the norms become incorporated into his behaviour; an old one is dropped, a new one is added. This is true of many learning experiences.

When you're first learning something new, it's very uncomfortable. Only when you do it for a while does it become more comfortable, to the point where you can do it without even thinking about it.

'The more and more you do something, soon it becomes a habit, and a skill, and then it sinks out of your conscious mind, and you do it naturally. Driving is a perfect example. At one point in our lives, for those of us who drive, we had to pay attention to everything. Now we drive and our minds are not even on what we are doing, we just drive automatically, on autopilot.'

For Ron, putting an item on his 'List of Intentions' bridges the gap, bringing the need into his awareness so he can start to work on it.

Writing Affirmations vs. Speaking Them

Ron writes the same things every day partly as affirmation, but also, he says, 'as a focusing thing and a memory thing'. The 'List of Intentions' helps him remember the kind of person he is striving to be. It is an umbrella, cumulatively creating an attitude, a foundation.

'These reminders set a pattern for me for when I go out into the world. Then I go out with a focus. I intend to do these things, I intend to monitor my thoughts, to be here and now, and to minimize the size of the food portions I eat, to talk less and listen more, and all the other things.'

And having the intention makes them more likely to happen.

'To write it out means I will live this way, this will be my focus. My pen could not copy anything I did not believe in. As I write each principle, I think about it, and test my commitment to it.'

Ron knows that many people might prefer to write up such a list as his once, or type it out, and then simply reread it every day, to reference the concepts by hearing themselves say them out loud. That technique would not be as effective for him.

'The reason that I write it out every day is to find out how connected I am.'

The very act of writing it out makes him ask himself, Am I here and now?

'When I wake up I'm in a different state. I've come out of a dream state, and sometimes I'm scattered. Sometimes it takes me a little while to write that list because I can't think of them, even though I write them every day. It is a measure for me of how alert my mind is and how connected I am, how grounded on a particular day.

'If I am spacey or can't remember something and need to look at the previous day's intention sheet, then I know to take that lack of sharpness, edge or presence into account during the day, making adjustments when necessary.'

Feeding the Inner Mind

Ron believes that writing it down feeds the inner mind, the 'other-than-conscious' mind.

'A vividly imagined image with emotional content is as strong as an actual experience as far as the brain and the "other-than-conscious" mind is concerned. By constantly feeding things to my "other-than-conscious" mind, I provide the universe with descriptions of the things that I am requesting of the world. That's another reason I write these items down every day.'

The 'list of intentions' has become for Ron a way to organize and arrange processes of accelerated learning and apply them to his daily behaviour.

'The benefits for me come in the depth and the richness of my life.'

• NOW YOU •

For Ron, writing his goals and principles down every day is a way of imprinting them on his behaviour; it influences his life. For him it is like brushing his teeth and washing his face every morning; he just does it, and it wakes him up for the day ahead. His list is personal and has meaning and application for him.

Create your own list of what is meaningful to you.

We often come across pithy aphorisms and striking concepts in our reading or conversation, or in taking a course. We see the wisdom of the notion and nobly pledge to incorporate its insight into our daily living.

All too soon it is forgotten before we have practised it enough to make it a habit.

Make your own 'List of Intentions' and begin your day by writing them out. It need not be from memory.

As you move into competence in one area, drop the saying you don't even have to think about any more, and add another maxim.

The benefit when you do this will come in the depth and richness of your life.

11

BECOMING COMMITTED

In an oft-quoted passage from *The Scottish Himalayan Expedition*, W. H. Murray speaks about the significance of commitment. Once you walk forward in faith with a conscious effort, all manner of support and tangible backing will be available to you.

> *Until one is committed, there is hesitancy . . . The moment one definitely commits oneself, then Providence moves, too. All sorts of things occur to help one that would never otherwise have occurred. A whole stream of events raising in one's favour . . . unforeseen incidents and meetings and material assistance which no man could have dreamed would have come his way.*

It is up to you to trust the possibility enough to be willing to put your dream in writing and to take the first step, even with no evidence that your dream will actually happen.

Bill's Story

My good friend Bill was having recurring dreams – not really nightmares, but sometimes they woke him up in the middle of sleep or left him feeling uneasy when he woke up in the morning.

His thirtieth college reunion from Rensselaer Polytech Institute in Troy, New York, was coming up, and the dreams were about school.

'A lot of people have dreams like this occasionally, dreams when you can't find the class, you can't find your locker, you don't remember if you did the homework. The difference was I started having them all the time.'

Bill is an easygoing kind of fellow, with an incisive mind and dry wit – the milieu at Rensselaer Polytech, considered one of the finest engineering science schools in the United States, suited him just fine.

Bill remembers his college years fondly: the fraternity parties, the camaraderie, the school spirit. He laughs at the memory of the time the whole town converged and tore the goalpost down for a tie game; it was the football team's first non-loss in four years.

He wanted to go back, it was important to him, but at the same time he did not think it was possible. Since he lives on the West Coast, the plane fare would be expensive and then he'd have to rent a car and get a hotel. His wife Dorothy's business was expanding and they were sinking a lot of their finances into it.

'Money was tight. A trip back East seemed out of the question.'

Bill decided building up Dorothy's business was more significant than his desire to attend his reunion.

And then the dreams started.

'Even though I had a very positive experience in school, the dreams were scary. Like, we're getting ready for the final exam and I don't know where the classroom is. And I didn't remember studying, even taking any classes. Then there was the locker dream which went like this: I had a locker where I had my books. There were walls and walls of lockers and I couldn't remember which one was mine. But I need to find the locker, because all the information is in there, including the book that tells me where the class is, which I don't remember.'

Bill also had dreams where he was walking through neighbourhoods, trying to find the school, and the fraternity was on the top of an elevated highway.

'The funny part was the dream landscape had nothing to do with the way things were. In real life, the fraternity is located on a plateau part of the campus. But the sense in the dream was that it was inaccessible or scary. Or that I was trying to reach something and couldn't get it.'

Then he had dreams where there were parties going on upstairs in the fraternity house. He could hear them, but not find them. He had trouble finding his way around.

All of the dreams had in common dark locked rooms, a mysterious unused stairwell and a big heavy door. 'I felt something cryptic about that door, like it was an arcane, closed-off place.'

The dreams were all about secret passages or finding places, even the locker dream, but Bill is not sure what the metaphor was for any of the dreams.

'If I had to guess, I would guess searching for the locker, not being able to find the class, the locked door and closed stairwell all had to do with finding my way in life.'

BILL WENT through the letters that the reunion committee sent to him about the big event and put the red-and-white 'Save This Date' magnet on his refrigerator. Then he got a call from his friend Jeff, his classmate and fraternity brother. Jeff was part of the group putting together the reunion for the class.

Bill told Jeff he wanted to go, but he didn't think he could manage it financially. Jeff said, 'Well, think about it. I'll put you down as "maybe".'

'The more I thought about it, the more I wanted to be there, and the more impossible it seemed.

'I kept telling myself that I had to do this.'

Write It Down

It was Dorothy who suggested to Bill that he write down his intention. So he did. A single sentence in an old journal.

> *This is what I want to accomplish: I want to return to Rensselaer for my 30th reunion.*

'I wrote it in my journal. Yeah, I have a journal — which I write in every six or seven years.'

He laughs.

'I'm big on journalizing.'

The time approached when Bill had to make a final decision. Even though they still didn't have the money, the deadline came, and Bill told Jeff, 'Yes, I'll be there. I'm coming, I'm going to do it. Put me down as a definite.'

And he sent the deposit for the dinner.

'So I committed to be there.'

He sniffs and shakes his head, still somewhat incredulous about how he took the decisive step of assent, without a clue as to how he would pull it off.

What Opened Up

It was getting closer and closer to the date; it got to the point where he had to purchase plane tickets. The reunion was in a few weeks. He was still trying to figure out how he was going to pay for the airfare, hotel and car rental.

Meantime Dorothy was juggling the books for the business. One day, she was bemoaning the huge phone bill when her eye caught a notice at the bottom of the bill about the long-distance charges being linked to frequent flier miles. She called the airlines and found a way to combine the phone points with what she had already earned in skymiles.

Between the two systems, they had enough miles to arrange for the ticket.

After that, things started happening fast.

When his brother John, who lives on New York's Long Island, heard that Bill wanted to go back for his reunion, he said he had an extra car.

By coincidence, John had just bought a truck; otherwise he would have needed his car to get to work.

'Now I could fly into New York City and drive upstate, which is a heck of a lot easier than trying to fly into a little place like Troy.'

There were more surprises in store. Bill's parents, who live in North Carolina, heard he was going back. They sent him a letter with a large cheque, saying 'Have a good time; here's some money.'

'I wasn't expecting that at all. It was generous of them. And it was out of the blue.

'And then his college chum Jeff said, "Don't bother about a hotel; you can stay with me."'

Now he had everything he needed.

The Reunion

Bill was met at the airport by his brother John and he visited with family before heading north to the reunion. He linked up with his pal Jeff, and together they went to the fraternity house.

When he got there, he knew his way around instantly.

And he knew the people, even the ones who at first looked quite different. No matter what the exterior, people didn't change that much inside.

'I know people grow. Dorothy and I have been married for twenty-seven years. Our relationship has grown and we've changed a lot. Yet what I learned, going back to seeing my old classmates, was yes, you probably do grow and change, but there is something in your personality that doesn't change. Your sense of humour, or lack of it, the way you look at life in general, and the way you interact with other people – there are certain basic things about you that just don't change. Of the people that were at the reunion, all were pretty much the same in some fundamental way. Their personalities were the way they were thirty years ago.

'There is security in that, because you can look at yourself and say, "I am the same person. I haven't become a different person." I can look at these people, and say, "Yes, Jeff is still Jeff; Dave is still Dave." Good for them. And I can look at myself and say, "I'm still me."

'It is a reassurance to know that people don't change. That tells you that there is something in each of us, as an individual, that is all our own.'

Why Write?

Bill likens writing down his goal to an article he read recently about engineers building bridges. The author of the piece poses the question, What makes the difference between somebody who fantasizes something and somebody who uses their imagination?

'The answer is, commitment. An engineer uses his imagination to design something with the idea of bringing it to reality. When you fantasize, there is no commitment to creating it, whereas when you imagine something with a personal commitment, it gets built. The distinction is commitment. What writing it down did was it got me out of fantasy to the level of commitment.

'There is a solidity in actually committing it to paper. It is a physical thing to put it on paper. Not a lot of people write. For me to write it down is an unusual event. Writing something down is a commitment.'

A Completion

After he came back from the reunion, Bill felt like he had fulfilled some kind of obligation.

'I had gone back and checked the reality against the dream.

I'm glad I went. There were not any secrets that I found out about myself or anyone else. It was more of a completion, like I was supposed to go.'

And after he went, the dreams stopped.

• NOW YOU •

The first step of commitment is to be willing to write down what you want. Then take some small action towards the realization of that dream, even in the face of evidence to the contrary. And then don't be surprised when support comes from unlikely places.

As Julia Cameron puts it in *The Artist's Way*, 'Leap, and the net will appear.'

12

STACKING GOALS:
RAISING THE BAR

Y ou can have more than one goal at a time, and let the success of one be the foundation for another. A bonus awaits you when you conquer a fear or master a skill. Often you get two for the price of one, as a growth you make in one area of your life shows up as a strength in another.

Marc's Batting Cage Story

Because he started late in singing, my friend Marc, who I write about in chapter 2, felt he had a lot to catch up on.

'I was afraid all the time of what was going to happen. Painstakingly, I stopped doing other things I enjoyed, put my nose to the grindstone, and worked at learning how to sing. I went about it very badly, from a logical left-brained, "first-things-first" kind of approach. Eventually it started to pay off, but it can take you just so far when you do things that way.'

When he was offered a major part at a major house, he was both thrilled and frightened.

'I had a crisis before I went to do that gig. Essentially, I was on the verge of having a career. Going there could move me forward, in terms of me letting go, and it scared me. I was scared, scared, scared.'

Marc decided to confront his performance anxiety by encountering head-on his fear of sports.

To understand the background of how he solved the problem and broke through the crisis, you need to know that when Marc was a kid growing up, he was never good at baseball, and was often the last one chosen for teams at school.

'I was a horrible athlete, very self-conscious. When they were drawing up sides, I was always picked last. One year, a kid in a body cast was chosen to play ahead of me.'

Marc decided to combat this old ghost with a decisive present-day action. He went with some friends to a batting cage to hit baseballs.

By the end of the day, Marc felt his confidence and competence growing. And his hunch was right; the experience in the batting cage spilled over to his singing.

The first time into the cage he actually hit the ball a couple of times, which was a huge surprise to him. The third time into the cage he hit the ball twelve out of sixteen times.

'It was the third time into the cage that I knew I could sing better.'

Now Marc looks for ways to stretch all the time. If he goes into a restaurant and the waitress suggests trying squid as a sushi appetizer, he is willing to order it, even if it is new to him and he might be afraid he won't like it.

'I do that more and more, challenge myself to do things

I've never done before; constantly try to move out of my comfort zone – try the thing on the menu I have not tried before just to try it. Because I know that every time I do that, I get a little better as a singer, because I get a little braver.'

Expanding Childhood Limitations

Doing something that seems insurmountable often has to do with defying childhood injunctions. We get to go back and contradict those childhood limits and rewrite the rules. There has to be a willingness to do it poorly at first and give yourself a pat on the back for doing it at all.

'Anything worth doing is worth doing – full-stop,' as my friend Carol Keeffe likes to say.

Janine once used an expression of how something was 'stuck in my head even though I did not know it was in my head'. She was referring to that magical subliminal way that things happen when we write them down and forget about them. There is a flipside to the phenomenon. Negative phrases like 'I can't do this'; 'They'll laugh'; 'Let me help' (even under the guise of kindness, it only implies that you are doing it all wrong); and 'You'll fail' get ingrained deep in our psyches, messages that get stuck in your head even though you don't know they are in your head.

Now that you are grown up, you can set the record straight.

We each have our own stumbling blocks; what is easy for one person might be a formidable task for another.

Last Hallowe'en, I carved a pumpkin for the first time in my life. In the past, I always thought everyone could carve better than I, so I let them do it. Or if I tried it and messed it up, or even hesitated, it was, 'Here! Let me do that!' taking the knife out of my hand.

On Hallowe'en, my sons, James and Peter, invited me over. They had purchased pumpkins, spread out the newspaper and they insisted, 'Here's the knife, you're doing your own.'

At first I was intimidated. I knew it would not be as inventive as theirs, because they are marvellously clever. I did it anyway. I made a Chinese one in honour of Puccini's *Turandot*. It wasn't very good, but it was mine. It felt freeing and fun.

The happiness I felt, the sense of accomplishment, spilled over into my next workday. I smiled broadly every time I thought of it.

Now I use that accomplishment as a metaphor for other things in my life. When I felt overwhelmed by a recent major move, Janine gave me a picture of a little girl carving a huge pumpkin, with a big grin on her – and the pumpkin's – face. I slapped it up on my refrigerator with a magnet and looked at it every day before tackling the moving boxes, the closets of stuff to discard, the attic of accumulated paper-work, the garage full of car and garden tools.

The picture said, 'You can do this (and it's fun!).'

Transferring Success

My friend Bob McChesney calls it 'stacking'. One success becomes leverage for the next.

Learning to use a computer back when that was a new concept helped me in my writing. There were those who said, 'You'll never be able to figure it out, you are too right-brained.'

Looking back now, I remember appreciatively how helpful my friend Bill Harrison was.

When I couldn't get the computer to do what I wanted, Bill used to say, 'What does the computer think you asked it to do?' Bill explained that whenever something went 'wrong', it was 'right' for the computer. I later heard this approach described with a fancy name: 'emphatic identification', which means becoming one with the machine you are trying to master; getting inside its 'head'. It is a secret tool many mechanically inclined people use when troubleshooting.

The point is, I did learn to use a computer, and doing that made me a sharper writer. Not because I now could drag down a thesaurus, or because word processing made deletions easy and moving blocks around smooth, but because the confidence I gained in my own ability to think had a lateral transfer to my creative work. I became more logical and organized my ideas better.

Coining a Metaphor

Here is a stacking story that continues to colour a whole life. An accomplished friend of mine takes on new challenges so confidently, I once asked her where she got her fearlessness from. Edna told me it had to do with something that happened when she was a young girl. She had seen a performer on TV riding a unicycle and she got it into her head that that was a splendid, magnificent kind of thing to be able to do. Such balance, such grace, such freedom and insouciance – no bars for hands to steer, unrestricted and free. The person on the unicycle looked so happy – even smug and natural. It looked easy.

Edna rented a unicycle from a cycle shop. That's when she found out it was not as easy as it looked. She kept falling off.

She kept at it and got better and better although still a little wobbly. She got good enough to convince her parents to buy her her very own unicycle for a birthday present. Now she could practise to her heart's content.

Soon Edna was as casual as the man on TV appeared, riding down to the library, to the store for her mum (with a satchel over one shoulder to carry back books or groceries), to a friend's house after school. It was as natural as walking, only speedier and more fun. She liked the way the wind ran through her hair as she pedalled along. She liked the smiles of passers-by and the animated pointing of young children as she rode past. She liked the manœuvreability and the way she could hop on and go.

Mostly, she was proud of herself for doing something she did not know she could do. It became emblematic of her drive and ability.

When Edna was studying French years later and having a tough time of it, her mother said, 'A girl who could ride a unicycle could learn French!' So she persevered and soon was doing so well in her French class the teacher asked her to tutor others.

She wanted a job after school, a part in the spring play; it became a familiar refrain, a cheer: 'A girl who could ride a unicycle could get a job like that, could audition and get picked, could act, could–, could–, could–, whatever.'

Edna laughs now to remember it. After a while, the significant triumphs that built on that one girlhood feat could have replaced it many times over as a milestone to measure other challenges by, but she always kept that one as her mantra.

And of course there were things she tried that did not work out, but she never paid much attention to those. A girl who can ride a unicycle knows she has options.

Putting a Man on the Moon

What does putting a man on the moon have to do with fighting global hunger? Rhetoricians would say, correctly, it is a 'false analogy'; that is, comparing two activities that are alike in trivial ways but dissimilar in significant ways. Oh well. The fact is that as a country, the USA has been motivated time and time again to do other great things because of that 'one small step for a man, one giant step for mankind'.

'A country that could put a man on the moon could . . .' And then they collectively figure out a way to do it.

It doesn't matter how tenuous the connection seems. What does riding a unicycle have to do with speaking French fluently? What does being in the batting cage have to do with singing well?

Nothing.

And everything.

This same mysterious connection happens when you begin writing things down and watch them happen. Synchronicity starts to inform all areas of your life. Soon the miracles are happening so fast you can hardly keep track of them.

• NOW YOU •

Write a list of the accomplishments in your life of which you feel especially proud. It could be something you did last week or something you did as a kid. Won a colouring contest. Swam the length of the pool. Got the promotion.

Use that list to choose your own private batting cage benchmark. Select one that resonates for you.

Or set out today to conquer a childhood block. Carve a pumpkin. Learn to bat. Take roller-skating lessons. Make it your mantra: 'A girl (or boy or man or woman) who could do that could do *anything*.'

If you have written a goal and made it happen, do another harder one, maybe in another part of your life. Or if you are stuck in a goal achievement as Marc was, try for another accomplishment in a totally different arena that will boost your confidence.

You just might get two – or more – for the price of one.

13

STARTING A GROUP: WHAT BY WHEN

If you are serious about having what you want in life, determine to meet systematically with like-minded people as a way to spur you on and assess your advancement. The deadline energy of having an appointment, with assignments due, can motivate completion and, by pointing out the progress you might have missed, give you an incentive to do even more.

At its best, such a group calls you to your highest ability and holds your vision even when your own sight dims.

The Seymour Group

For several years now, I have profited immensely by being part of The Seymour Group. The Seymour Group meets every week, once a week on Friday mornings at Vivace's. Or not.

We meet at precisely 8:00 A.M. The members are always punctual: they arrive exactly on time, ready to report on their week's assignments. Or not.

The members are scrupulous about keeping strictly to business, honouring each other's time, and rarely, if ever, bring up topics of a personal nature. Oh well. We try. And the point is that a group can be whatever you want it to be, whatever brings out the best in you.

If you form a group like ours, you might want to meet at exactly the same time each week and allow each person fifteen minutes of reporting on his or her goals, during which time no one else interrupts. You might want to use a timer for this, to make sure no one person holds the floor longer than another. After each member has his or her allotted fifteen minutes, you might consider a summary and projection of the week ahead, totalling ten minutes apiece, and again use a timer to keep everyone on track.

Then again, you might not.

Either way, whether you play by set rules or make up new ones as you go along, a regular goal gathering can be a dramatic guide through the nitty-gritty, step-by-step task of making wishes come true.

The Secret

The Seymour Group is the kind of loose-fitting team that works best for me. But I admit we are a bit unconventional.

The first convention we violate is that groups of this type ordinarily have four to eight members. The secret is (please don't tell anybody) there are just two of us, my friend Janine and me, and we like it that way. That way, if one or the other of us is late, or does not show up at all (which has happened on occasion), only one other person is inconvenienced and that other person is understanding and forgiving, because she was probably late or forgot to show up herself not so long ago. We have enormous patience with each other and allow all kinds of topics to crop up that are not on the agenda. It works for us. We have figured out how to combine fun with hard work.

Janine and I named our get-togethers 'Group' so you wouldn't know our club only has two members, and called it The Seymour Group so it sounded as important as an investment meeting. Of course, it is an investment meeting, but the stock is in ourselves and the dividends pay a higher yield than most mutual funds.

Wishcraft

I sincerely believe that Barbara Sher herself would be delighted with our maverick club, even though she is the one who made up most of the standards we break every week (or every other week, depending on when we get together). Barbara Sher wrote the wonderful book *Wishcraft*, and I took a high-energy course from her years ago. Sher recommends meeting on a consistent schedule with what she calls 'success teams' to support each other in making dreams reality. In the years since taking Sher's motivating class, I have both formed and joined several different 'success teams'. All of these teams contributed to my life, and I am grateful to them.

No matter how the make-up of these groups varied, two underlying premises remained the same:

1) If you are headed in the right direction, all you need to do is keep on walking.
2) It's nice to have others who believe in you walking alongside, making suggestions, encouraging you on.

THE SETUP is simple. Each week in a little memo book, write down your respective mini-goals, the piece of the puzzle that will eventually make the big picture: 'By next week I will . . .'

And then copy, as well, the other people's promises. This not only makes each of you committed, it also makes you accountable.

What? By When?

To my mind, the two most important questions you can ask a person who is serious about moving forward in a project, any project, are:

1) What will you do next?
2) By when will you do it?

And the third key ingredient is the principle of
'Return and Report'

When I use this formula to challenge someone outside of The Seymour Group as a 'one time only' inducement to action, I often add, 'Call me when you have done it.' And this one *is*, as Sher suggests, strictly a business call. Hang up and call back if you want to chat.

Recently I was speaking with a young woman who was ready to claim her goal. She was clear what the next step would be, yet I startled her by asking, pointblank,

'OK, by when will you do that?'

With great enthusiasm, she answered confidently, 'Soon!'

She felt proud of herself, so imagine her surprise at my rejoinder,

'"Soon" is not an answer. By *when* will you do it?'

Now she was more tentative.

'Sunday? I guess I could do that by Sunday.'

'OK. Will you call me on Sunday and leave a message on my machine telling me that you did that?'

She did and she did.

When 'Return and Report' is, by agreement, an ongoing arrangement, like the regular meetings of The Seymour Group, then the next step, after the report, is to throw the marker out a little farther and challenge each member to swim towards the new microgoal.

'OK, you sent for the catalogue. By next week, will you call the dean of Admissions and get a registration form?'

'Congratulations. You got the classical guitar you have been coveting. How many hours will you put in next week for lessons and practice?'

Keeping Your Eye Upon the Donut

I know a new dad who wrote a letter to his just-born son. 'Let the rest of the world be the heavy. I want to be your champion.'

Your goal group needs to offer that kind of unconditional bias. A goal group is no place for 'tough love' or ultimat-

ums. It is a fan-to-fan forum where the key is positive rein-
forcement.

Janine is a good example of this for me. She is natural
and easygoing – and maternal. I like that. She claps at even
my baby steps.

When it seems as though I am going nowhere, Janine is
quick to say, 'Look what you did! OK, so you didn't accomplish A, B and C – we'll put those on the list for next week.
But give yourself some credit, you *did* do D, E and F. Nice
work.'

My dear dad taught me a lesson I sometimes forget. A
jingle he was fond of spouting epitomizes his philosophy on
life:

> *As you amble on through life, friend,*
> *Whatever be your goal–*
> *Keep your eye upon the donut*
> *And not upon the hole!*

A good goal group will acknowledge what is, rather than
dwell on what isn't. You begin to see how it all fits together.
One foot after the other. The stumbling baby steps become
a steady walk.

Chip! chip! chip!, the résumés are done and in the post,
the attic cleaned; the house is ready to go on the market,
the sorting boxes properly filed, the dreaded phone call
placed and successful.

'By next week, I will . . .'

Week after week, step by step. The new small business is
successfully launched, the trip taken, the foreign language
facilitated. The walk turns to a run as you triumphantly cross
the finishing line and, hardly hesitating, look around for the
next challenge.

Rising to the Challenge

When I say that Janine is 'easygoing' I don't mean 'easy'. Janine demands a lot of me, and I in turn help raise her bar. You can do the same with your group.

The Seymour Group often challenges each other to stretch, to reach higher than what we think we can do. I constantly come up with plans for Janine that seem impossible in the allotted time frame, and she in turn spurs me on to do the undoable with her pet phrase – said with a sweet smile that disarms the stern schoolmarm tone. Quite matter-of-factly, with raised eyebrows and a motherly, up-and-down nod of the head, she says, 'You can do this.'

The impression I am left with is strong: Someone else has confidence in me; why shouldn't I?

We Go Way Back

The longer your group continues to meet, the more bolstering you can be. You can remind each other of past conquests as 'batting cage' benchmarks for future triumphs.

Two years ago Janine and I together did the 'Three-Day Novel Writing Contest' that I mentioned previously in Ron's story and talk about in *Put Your Heart on Paper*. We often reference that to reinforce our respective resolve.

'A girl who could write a novel in three days could . . .'

The next trick is to break down big chunks of challenge into controllable segments.

Janine wanted to enter the annual two-hundred-mile 'S-T-P' (Seattle-to-Portland) bike ride.

A girl who could write a novel in three days could do that!

All she has to do is break the training down into manageable parts and write down one piece at a time.

Janine knew she could go ten miles at a stretch, and there was a loop, right near her home, to Seward Park and back, which was ten miles.

I challenged her to pedal that path seven times between our present meeting and the next one.

'Five times is reasonable; anything more would be a bonus.'

'OK. Fifty miles biking by next week, for sure – aim for seventy.'

She wrote down:

Fifty miles biking, ten miles at a time, by next week.

'This is good. This makes it possible, in small bites.'

'T.T.T.'

Janine and I have been meeting regularly for almost three years. I have filled four or five memo books, including a small gilded one from Florence. ('Meet Emily in Italy' was one of my goals, broken down into manageable parts.) When I read over the weekly bullets in those books, I see how commitment plus accountability helped Janine to first finish and then submit her historic novel for publication, bike that two-hundred-mile S-T-P, plan a romantic weekend getaway with her husband, propose and receive a grant for an in-service curriculum on harassment for the school district, enter her photography in a national contest, and approach a millionaire for a donation to help publish a memoir book for her senior students.

For my part, The Seymour Group got me back to Greece, pushed me to proceed in a lawsuit (I won!), guided me in hiring office staff, and got me to propose and write this book, story by story, chapter by chapter. Write one chapter, edit three; proofread; draw up table of contents, edit changes, enter; write new, bit by bit, and here it is – this book itself is a tribute to The Seymour Group and 'steady on'.

Those memo books are a treasure to me. They show me the steps that got me where I want to be – over and over and over. They remind me, as my friend John Garner likes to say, 't.t.t.t.' ('these things take time'). They provide a record of the persistent perspiration that goes along with initial inspiration. Looking back on the weekly challenges checked off shows how we came to this point, the conquests along the way, the building blocks carefully put in place.

Because Janine and I have so much *fun*, it doesn't feel like work – but then I look with astonishment at all we accomplish directly because of meeting.

Completion creeps up on you. The important thing is to do *something* – anything that propels you forward, keeps the dream fresh in your reticular activating system, so you will be attuned to signs, start collecting evidence. You can do this. Before you know it, you are sipping wine on a sidewalk café in Paris, or taking orders, fast and furious, for your new business. You are so busy enjoying yourself, you might forget there was ever a time when you thought it was not possible.

• NOW YOU •

Read Barbara Sher's *Wishcraft*. Form a goal group that reflects your own best style. There is no right or wrong way to do it. Cheer each other on as you take the steps that will eventually lead to completion of your dreams. Each week, ask each other, 'What will you do by next week to further your goal?' Write it down, then 'return and report' the following week. Before you know it, your old goals will be history and you will be setting new ones. You will have climbed every mountain you dreamed of and be scaling heights you never thought possible.

Trust me.

You can do this.

14

TAKING THE INITIATIVE

My children always loved the story of Dumbo the Flying Elephant; they begged me to read it to them over and over again. You remember the plot: Everyone made fun of the elephant with the big ears until he was befriended by a mouse who gave him a magic feather. With this feather, Dumbo could fly.

Now he was soaring and wowing the crowds. Those who derided him were applauding wildly – he was confident and free – until *he dropped the feather*. Immediately, Dumbo plummeted towards the ground and was heading for a crash when the mouse, who was along for the ride, shouted in his ear, 'Dumbo! It's not the feather – it's you. You know how to fly!'

Hearing that, Dumbo righted his course and was able to continue soaring – on his own powers.

When you write down your aspirations, it is true that support often comes from unpredictable outside sources and yet, especially if you are stuck on a goal, don't lose sight of the implied imperative in the title of this book: *(You) Write It Down, (You) Make It Happen.* It's not a magic feather, it's you.

Sometimes in order for your dream to come true, it is you who need to take the initiative.

Marian's Story

One autumn day my office phone rang. A woman who lived in Wells, Nevada (population 1,000) was calling. Her name was Marian. Marian had read *Put Your Heart on Paper* (three times, she told me), and wanted to know if there was any chance I might come to Wells, America's cowboy poetry outpost, to do a workshop. We got to talking; it felt like we knew each other, like we were old friends. Quite easily, she was soon telling me a remarkable story about an impossible dream come true, one that she wrote down before it happened.

Marian and her husband are ranchers. They live in an area so remote that their address has an HC – 'Highway Contract' – number. That means that since neighbours are so far apart, the post office contracts out the mail delivery to a private carrier. There is only one grocery store in Wells; in fact, the only shopping in town is this one store, it is a chemist and grocery store combined. Any other shopping means a drive to Twin Falls two hours away, or Elko, just over an hour.

In a strong yet soft voice that spoke volumes in its tone, Marian filled me in on some background.

'You have to know our history; my husband and I feel as if we've been with pre-school children all of our lives.

We had eight children of our own, and then we adopted two. We home-schooled our last three children.'

When Marian speaks of pre-schoolers in the house, she is not referring simply to the children, though. It is her tender way to describe the sense of responsibility she and her husband felt while caring for their ageing parents, as well.

Marian's mother has Alzheimer's, so Marian knows first-hand the deep sadness and helplessness – and even the frustration and resentment – that comes from watching someone you love, someone once sharp and vibrant and self-sufficient, slip into dementia and needing more care than you can provide.

So she felt personally the need for families to have help with their elderly.

'Taking care of ageing parents is confining. It's not that people don't want to do it. Others often make that judgement. Those who judge don't understand sometimes how difficult it is to take care of the elderly or even to be close to them.

'Even a loving and giving daughter or son is frightened to think that they could never be independent again, never go on a trip again without their sick mother or father with them.

'I know those feelings. I know how difficult it is to have someone with you all the time. But I also know how awful it is to feel that you are not doing your duty, that you are selfish enough to want a life of your own and want some independence and some freedom.'

Marian wrote of this dichotomy in her journal,

> *Mum fell this morning. We heard a thud on the monitor
> we keep beside her bed. I don't know how to make it safer*

*for her. She is so frail and ill-looking. But she can be wilful
and bossy and demanding, too. Sometimes she is gentle
and grateful, also. I must learn to ignore the bad times and
cherish and remember the good.*

*How do other families cope? For many it is not pos-
sible to give up their work and their personal lives to
care for an aged parent. Where can they turn for help?
Who will help us?*

Searching for a Place

As she sat in hospital waiting rooms or doctors' offices
through a series of major illnesses leading up to the final
diagnosis of Alzheimer's disease, many times Marian wrote
out her dream of a place that could provide for her mother
a 'family away from family'. At one point, Marian went with
her sisters to Salt Lake City to look at some facilities for
seniors that were recommended to her.

*Jane and Ann think it is time for Mum to move to a rest home.
I'm not so sure of that, but I looked anyway. The City Care Centre
and Upland Cove both are possibilities, but they lack so much.
They are both large facilities, looking and smelling like charity
hospitals. The personnel were friendly, and on first appearance seemed
to care for the elderly. But there are so many old people there and
it is so impersonal! Long, cold halls, so many wheelchairs, such a
feeling (was it only me?) of waiting for the inevitable – death.*

Simultaneous entries in her journal show her question-
ing her own place in the world, asking, '*Now what? What is
my purpose? What is it that I am to do at this point in my life?*'

She describes her plight in a picturesque way.

'I had this strong feeling that I was at the crossroads. I wrote that so many times in my journal. I was stuck, sitting under the sign, with my backpack on my back, waiting for direction.'

MARIAN continued to dream on paper of a home where families could get assistance, where they knew that their parents would be well taken care of. Not an institution or a nursing home, not a facility, but a home, a place where there were loving people who could care for them and could socialize with them, talk with them and hear their stories – and at the same time, provide the physical care that was needed.

Marian laughs and says, 'So out of that was born the idea that *someone* should do something, but I did not ever think of it as being me.'

Little did Marian realize that the personal direction she sought would synchronize with her need to ease her mother's plight.

Pointing Back to Her

A chance conversation with a son-in-law was the first inkling that in order to make this particular dream happen, Marian might have to take the initiative herself. Out of the blue, without knowing about her longings, or what she had written, her son-in-law said to her one day, 'Have you ever thought about building a retirement home?'

A friend of his had been in contact with a company called

Bee Hive Development, a new group that built small, family-type homes for seniors around the country. Their idea was born out of the same need as Marian's – the two partners had family members who needed help.

Marian made a call, then another and another. She had to make a dozen calls to track down the two partners. Then things started hopping.

'Within the week, the CEO of the company had met with me and we began talking about it. I loved the concept and I loved the fact that they said that they would never build a bigger home than one which cared for nine residents. Despite the fact that you can run an eighteen-bed facility much more inexpensively per person than you can the eight- or nine-bed, they promised they would never enlarge. Nine is still like a family.

'We began talking about the possibility of building such a place in Nevada.'

Marian was still reluctant, wishing someone else would build the home. She did not know the first thing about architects and building permits, let alone running such a place. It took great courage for her to start. She had to break new ground every day; dealing with difficult contractors and bureaucratic government officials called for a toughness that was not her style. She had to work through a maze of rules and regulations that the state required, as well as defend herself against the sceptics and naysayers who said the town did not have enough of a population base to sustain such an undertaking.

But there was no getting around it; everything kept coming back to her being the one to do this.

'It seemed like something had taken over. We could not get permission to build anywhere we looked in the larger communities, so finally we decided to come back here.'

Six months after the conversation with her son-in-law, they opened the door to the first residents. Marian says proudly, 'It is a beautiful building, state-of-the-art for that purpose. My thing is decorating and so it's lovely, with warm pictures and colours. Every room is embellished a little differently. The nicest thing about it, though, is that the building itself has a welcoming warmth about it.'

Little miracles seem to happen at the Bee Hive Home. A man came who had a well-earned reputation for being difficult. He had been an alcoholic and had a foul mouth, returning meanness for kindness at every turn. Yet, poignantly, after two weeks, he told Marian, 'I recognize you. Don't leave me.'

One of the women they took in complained about everything. She commandeered the remote control and put herself in charge of the TV. She didn't like this, wouldn't do that.

'But now,' Marian says, 'she has mellowed. Her son told us, "I've never seen this side of her before." I'm not saying she has changed completely, she can still be very rough; but she is more compassionate.'

Capturing and Preserving National Treasures

When Marian compared ageing parents to pre-schoolers, she meant it as an attitude to help understand and appreciate seniors' clumsiness and distraction, and to be prepared for their unexpected, sometimes humorous utterances. We don't require pre-schoolers to do everything right, to even feed themselves correctly. They often do embarrassing things in public, make inappropriate loud noises, or make a big mess and we don't mind. Marian suggested approaching the way the elderly act, and the curious way they look at the world, with the same sense of patience and enjoyment.

By way of example, she tells a story about her own mother, who she says is both elegant and imperious.

'My mother is quite tall, beautifully dressed, and absolutely loco right now. Yet she does have these moments when she is right on. There is a day person who prepares the meals and an evening person who serves the main meal. Mother came and sat down at the dinner table and looked around, and said, "Well, they've done their research."'

'Virginia, another resident who is caustic, said, "What do you mean, Lillian?" and Mother said, "Well, they found out everything I hate and they served it all in one meal."'

Or the time someone asked Hazel, the oldest resident, if she wanted to go out, and she said, 'I am not sticking my beak out of this building until I've seen the first robin.'

Marian laughs softly.

'The staff and I share comments like this with each other and we are constantly delighted by them.'

Many of the residents also provide a classic view into life a long time ago.

Hazel is 101 years old. She rarely says more than one word at a time. But on 2 February, she blurted out, 'My boy Doug was born on Groundhog Day.'

Encouraged by the staff, she poured out a marvellous story of Doug's birth, a wonderful tale of good neighbours pulling together, pulling for this little baby to be born. There was a raging blizzard and Hazel's husband, George, had to travel over sixty miles by horse to Elko, across the Ruby Mountains, through Secret Pass along steep and winding roads, to get the doctor. All along the way there were fresh horses waiting for him at the ranches he passed.

The return journey was marked by the same neighbourliness. In Hazel's words,

> *He gathered up Old Doc Hood; no, not young Tom, but Tom's grandfather, borrowed a buggy, and started back for the ranch. There were teams and wagons stationed all along the way. George and Doc changed outfits and kept on a' comin'. I was mighty glad to see 'em both. It was only a few more hours and we had us a baby boy. His dad was sure proud of him.*

When Helen, another resident who has no children, heard Hazel tell this story, she said, 'You sure were in labour a long time.' Marian smiled as she wrote down Hazel's response,

> *It was worth it. He's a good boy.*

Hazel's boy Doug is eighty-two now, and they typed up this story and gave it to him. You are never too old to know your dad was proud of you and your mum thinks you were worth the pain of labour.

After giving Hazel's story to Doug, Marian got together with her staff and decided to add something to their mission statement. Marian explained, 'We are required by law to keep a daily log, mostly to correspond with each other about what happened that day. I said to my staff, "Let's make this a real log; let's write down in dialogue the funny little conversations that take place, or the poignant things we hear."

'Now our mission statement says our purpose is threefold: to provide physical care, to provide a loving family atmosphere, and third, to write down the memories of these people who are a national treasure. They need and deserve to have their stories told.'

The plan is to get them to tell their tales, write them down, and give them in booklets to their relatives.

Knowing It Was Meant to Be

One of the best things that has come from this, Marian told me, is the response from the community.

'So many people said, "Nothing good ever happens in this little town," and now there is this to prove good things do happen here. People have been supportive and thrilled. When they come in to the building they gasp, because it is so nice. They didn't expect that we would do it here. And I can't blame them – I never suspected it myself.'

Marian is well aware what a tremendous gamble this undertaking is. They used every penny of their life savings to fund it. She worries about being able to make it financially, or at least breaking even.

'This is something I wanted to do, but I've had to second-guess my decision so many times.'

One night, after hours, something happened that convinced Marian she was doing the right thing. Something hard to put into words:

'One evening, I finally got my mother into bed. She does not sleep much, does not sit down much; she is constantly on the move. I knelt beside her bed to pray with her. Then I went into Helen's room to ask her if I could pray with her, and I did.'

Another resident, Angela, had been particularly agitated that day, opening and closing doors, holding imaginary conversations with her kittens and people from her past, obsessively wiping away non-existent spots in the bathroom sink. Marian spent a little extra time with her that night, to reassure and console her. One by one, she did the same with each of the other residents.

'I just talked with each of them, listening to their needs, talking with them about their feelings, about eternal things. I left the last room and started down the hall; the only light was from the little night-lights that flicker in the hallways. I had the most beautiful feeling of peace and comfort that I have ever experienced in my life. It was as if there were warm arms encircling the entire building.'

Marian called her husband right away.

'I phoned him and said to him, "Whatever happens, it's worth it. If we have to close the doors in a week, this one experience has been worth all of that."'

And she continues to have those feelings that it was meant to be and that it is a wonderful venture.

'I also hate it a lot of times because it is such a worry and there are those days, just like raising small children, that are so exhausting. But the bottom line is that it was a great thing to do and I'm glad we did it.'

Writing Set the Wheels in Motion

Although she was astonished at the way things unfolded, Marian was not surprised that writing it down was part of the process that set the wheels in motion. She sums it up by saying that when you write something down, you begin to define what you know and, therefore, what you want. You can't have what you want until you know what it is.

Writing clarifies what it is that you are asking for. God can give you what you want, says Marian, but you have to be clear on what you want.

And writing opened her up to the news that the first step would have to come from her. Marian used her journal as a place to collect the signs or signals that things were going well, that this was meant to be. That gave her the courage to act, knowing that if she took the risk, the backing would be there.

'That's another benefit of writing – it helps me to recognize what is happening and to appreciate it. When I don't write it down, sometimes I overlook those small victories and forget to be grateful.'

Writing gave her the courage to act.

Prophetic Pages

In the light of her remarkable achievement, it sends a chill down my spine to now read this description in Marian's journal pages, written over two years before her son-in-law approached her:

What I'd like to find is a small homelike facility where the staff could mingle with, eat with, as well as care for the elderly as if they were beloved parents and grandparents. The decor would be light and bright, colourful and warm, reminding the residents of their best-remembered days when they were young and productive. A place where memories are listened to, cherished, maybe recorded. Where mealtimes are presided over by someone who encourages conversation and interaction and laughter; where disabilities are minimized and abilities strengthened. A place where caregivers are more than employees, but are people filled with compassion and love and the knowledge that their personal lives will be blessed because of the care they give to those who need them so much. They will be people who willingly serve, knowing that their own old age needs will be graciously attended, and that when they enter into the world where we are ageless, they will be greeted and thanked by all those whom they helped. Perhaps I am senile and delusional myself to have such a wish.

Far from delusional, Marian expressed in her writing something her head did not yet know, but her heart knew deeply. In her longing, she anticipated the reality before it happened. And unwittingly, she also projected her own part in the undertaking. Almost four years before opening Bee Hive Home, Marian had written another prophetic entry in her journal notebook:

What is the best use of my life now? What is the highest good? I have asked myself that question since I was a youth and the answer is not forthcoming. At one time I thought I would do some remarkable deed that would benefit mankind and put my name in the history books. I soon outgrew that self-serving notion. I know whatever my work is will involve serving others and that the reward will be the quiet peace that accompanies such work.

Wells, Nevada. Population, 1,000. One small store, grocery and chemist combined. There is something else there now, too: a state-of-the-art nursing home with a hug around it.

• NOW YOU •

Next time you are writing out a description of the perfect achievement of your plan, go one step further and answer in writing the questions, 'Where do I fit into the equation? What do I need to do to help make this happen?'

Listen closely to the conversations around you, collect the signs and signals that might be challenging you to take the initiative.

It's not a magic feather; it's you who can fly.

15

WRITING LETTERS
TO GOD

The Middle Eastern expression 'From your lips to God's ears!' means 'May God hear your prayer.'

I say, 'From your pen to God's ears!'

And why not?

Praying on paper is a way of acknowledging God's presence in your life, asking for help and giving thanks.

Taped into one of my journals is a cocktail napkin from United Airlines with a phrase scribbled across it; it was the nearest thing to write on when I was in the friendly skies, watching the inflight movie *The Wedding Singer*. It is a sweet movie, but I wasn't paying too much attention to it until I heard this line sung in the background as the hero bemoans the loss of his sweetheart:

'I don't believe in an interventionist God.'

Maybe he didn't believe, but God intervened anyway – he got the girl he longed to marry.

I *do* believe in an interventionist God, a God who cares for me personally.

Sometimes it seems kind of silly; surely the Almighty has more pressing things on his agenda than your lost notebook, I tell myself. There are wars and famine and terrorist bombings and people in serious pain, emotional and physical.

Where in heaven does a letter like this go?

Dear God,

Please help me find my missing journal. It has a lot of important stuff in it. It is somewhere in your world — did I leave it at a coffee shop; wouldn't they call me? Or did they just toss it in a drawer waiting for me to ask? God, please help. You know where it is.

There must be a lost and found department in heaven, or maybe God gives the assignment over to a lower-level agent. I don't know. All I do know is that when I write letters to God, no matter how mundane they are, God answers his mail.

Letting the Pen Respond

Sometimes the answer comes through my writing, as a dialogue. I usually write to God at night before going to bed, and then, first thing in the morning, while I am only half-awake, I write out both sides of a conversation going on inside my sleepy head.

I write down the words as fast as they come to me, without stopping to edit or analyse.

I repeat the query from the night before; often I am startled by the directness of the response.

God, where is the letter from the programme director?

It is inside a bag — the black canvas bag under the desk.

Sometimes the reply is not what I want or expect, but there is always kindness and caring in it, like a loving parent, supportive but admonishing:

Is my journal in the car boot with my laptop?

No, it is not. I want you to finish writing this book. I will make that easy and flowing for you. Do not let anything stand in the way — not anything — let go of finding the journal — let go of wondering and worrying. Go to Vivace's and write! You can do it — and it will flow as soon as you give it the time — that's all that is needed. You will find what is missing after you reclaim, rediscover your own powers: All you need is within. Just write.

Any chance I could find the floppy disk — I know I entered so much on there.

It will come to you, don't waste time looking.

I did as I was told. I went back to my writing.
To my delight, both the disk and the journal did show up in the next few days.

Is It Your Own Subconscious Answering?

When you pose a question at night and get an answer in the morning, the doubter will say it is your own subconscious answering. That may be true, but then, too, maybe it is God leading you to the part of your subconscious that has the answer.

Before I dismiss the answers I get as simply my own imagination, I recall a dramatic incident that happened several years ago. I was scheduled to give a presentation to a large group of over four hundred people out of state; the sponsors had invited me to sell my books and any tapes I might have in the back of the room. They would even provide assistants to help me manage the money.

This was a great boon, but at the time I had no audiotape to sell. Then I remembered a programme I had done eight years earlier which had been taped. I realized the message of that tape would be perfect for this audience – but I only had one week to find it, duplicate it and package it. I had searched the family room, where we kept racks and racks of old motivational tapes and sales tapes, and even some tapes of radio interviews or other programmes I had done, none of which seemed right. I knew which tape I wanted, but I didn't have a clue where that tape could be; I only knew that it existed. I was feeling rather desperate, perhaps more so because I was worried about money; if I could find this tape, it would help me.

> *Dear God,*
> *I need to find the audio tape to copy for sale at the convention this weekend. Please tell me in writing tomorrow morning where to find it – directly – no time to waste – and also could you wake me up in time, feeling refreshed even though I am going to bed so late tonight?*
> *Thank you for my friends and my family who are like the Rock of Gibraltar in my life.*

Next morning, early, I pulled my journal into bed with me. I was still groggy, but I cut right to the chase.

OK, God. So where is the audiotape?

In the attic.

Huh? Not in the family room where all the tapes are?

In the attic.

I don't have any time to waste; I need it right now. The attic is a big place. Where in the attic?

I was getting annoyed. I was still sure it was in the family room and I was being sent on a wild-goose chase.

Look to the left.

C'mon. What do I look for?

A shoebox inside a bigger box. On the left, middle.

Still doubting and in my pyjamas, I went into the hallway and pulled down the spring ladder to the attic. I crawled up the steps, went on my knees along the left and there was a big box that I had not noticed before. I looked inside and found a shoebox of old tapes — among them, the tape I was looking for and needed.

This helpful message from God was particularly power-ful to me for several reasons. For one, I was at a low ebb in my life and it reminded me that God cares. For another,

I was able to duplicate that tape and sell over two hundred copies in the next two weeks; the income I received helped sustain me through a tough time.

Most significantly (I still haven't figured this part out), this answer belied my own cynicism that the answers from God are just me in an alpha state: I was not the one who had put that tape in the shoebox in the attic and I had no way of knowing it was there.

No way except one way.

Getting Answers Indirectly

If your letter is a petition, the answer does not always come through the next morning's writing. But if you have asked for it in prayer-writing, the return is forthcoming.

Years ago, my daughter Emily gave me a gift of a small pamphlet of about two dozen pages that she'd found on her travels. It was published in the 1920s and had a quaint way of using exclamation points and italics. There was much wisdom between the lines. I remembered that the author had made some succinct points about the power of writing down what you want. For the life of me, I could not recall where this book came from or how to locate another. I called several bookstores, but it was too tiny to be included in Books in Print so they could not order it. Since it was so old, there was a good chance it was out of print anyway.

I was not sure of the author's name, but the title was hard to forget. The publishers claimed the title came from an early response to the formula of the manuscript: *It Works!*

When all other avenues failed, I wrote a letter to God, mentioning the book by name and then leaving it in God's hands. I was confident that if locating that little book were important to my work, God would figure out a way to get me a copy.

As it turned out, it was what my cousin Larry calls 'a Zen find', that is, a totally unexpected perfect-fit connection, like finding a song you have been searching for in a bin at a used record store. Two weeks after I penned my request to God, a friend lent me an odd book, self-published in 1972, about how to win any contest you enter.

Plunked down in the middle of the text on a certain page, with no transition and no lead, seemingly as an after-thought, was a reference to *It Works!*, including ordering information.

I almost fell out of my chair. For the author of the contest book to mention this slight, seventy-year-old pamphlet was one thing, but to tell how to send away for it was pure serendipity.

Within the week, I had the copy I needed.

MY YOUNG friend Charlotte writes letters to God all the time, without expecting a written response. Charlotte is a neighbour of mine, a sixteen-year-old high school student. One day, she heard me talking to her mother about letters to God.

Shyly, she showed me some letters she herself had written, not only to God, but to a whole chorus of protectors.

I was touched when Charlotte told me I could share these letters. They have a depth in them I found both remarkable and stirring. In their innocence and beauty, they gently underscore the fact that prayer is like a conversation with a trusted, wiser friend.

Dear God,

Well, I call you today for extra assistance in the many things that are occurring in my life. There is no order of importance. I first ask you to help me become completely fit. That would entail losing a lot of weight and becoming a healthy eater as well as a regular exerciser. I know that it is in my possibility range, I could just use some help and motivation. I thank you for your assistance in the weight I have already lost.

Second, you know Deli-Boy who works in the grocery store? I know you know his name but that has not yet been for my discovery. I would ask that you help make him a reality for me. Out of all of my boys that I flirt with and what-not, I have the most healthy feeling about him. Please don't make this one a disappointment.

Third, I ask you to help me prepare fully for finals that are creeping up on me. Help me to stay focused and succeed in doing very well in my exams, and in my everyday school work.

I next ask you for the best possible summer job.

Lastly, I ask for your assistance in my new leadership position at school, help me to succeed and not stray. Help me to stay involved with others, but have a job and a life at the same time.

Thank you for listening to my prayer and I know it is a lot to ask but I know the best will always work out for me. It is now 11:05 and since I have to get up at 6:00 A.M. tomorrow, I'm going to say good night.

Love always and forever,

Charlotte Jean

Charlotte did not expect a direct answer, but she was confident her prayers were heard. A letter written several months later shows that her unblinking faith did not go unrewarded.

Dear God, Jesus, Mary and my Guardian Angels,

How are you? Well, while you're off making a difference in people's lives and environments I want to thank you for the difference you've made in mine. I was just looking back on my previous journal entries and Wow! It is amazing the difference you have made. I had a great summer. I went on two great retreats with my youth group and my typing job kept me flexible. Plus I improved my typing skills (something I thought was impossible). Who'da thunk? Also, to think I once called Brian 'Deli-Boy'. We are now friends and he likes me for who I am and I can definitely live with that, though more would never hurt (hint, hint). Also, I am doing great in school, even with my busy schedule. I am so blessed. I have a life and I'm doing well and keeping up.

Well, if it is not too much hassle I could still use a hand in losing weight. But at least I'm not self-conscious about it any more.

Well, anyway I love you tons & thanks,

Charlotte Jean

Giving Thanks and Praise

The letters Charlotte shared with me were also a reminder that prayer is not just supplication, but praise and thanksgiving. Not all letters to God are pleas for help.

I'd just like to take a moment to thank God, Jesus, the saints, Mary and my angels for getting me through a tough time in my life. For making it a spiritually strengthening experience. For always being there and listening to my prayers. For walking with me wherever I go and for holding my hand when I feel pain or when I am lonely. Thank you also for the beautiful surroundings around me. Especially rainbows and sunsets. I thank you for giving me the gift of my family and the wonderful people that support and encourage me. I thank you also for giving me a strong and wise spirit and I know that I can and will go a long way with it, but not of course without you as my leaders, companions and supporters. Thank you, thank you, thank you. Please, if there is something I can do to serve you, make it easy for me to do so. I am forever indebted to you. Love always, forever,

Charlotte Jean

Thanking You in Advance, I Remain . . .

Thanking God in advance for something not yet done is one of the highest forms of prayer. Implicit in such a prayer is the confidence that you are his child, and he would give you your heart's desire if only you tell him what you want.

'What father among you,' it says in the Gospel of St Luke, 'will give his son a snake if he asks for a fish, or hand him a scorpion if he asks for an egg?'

Humorist Marianna Nunes, a fellow member of the National Speaker's Association, wrote such an anticipatory letter to God, thanking him for the husband she did not yet have. The letter was born out of the frustration of trying to meet a partner through the conventional means available to modern singles. She was an avid reader of the personals, answering what must be a record seventy-four ads in two years.

She got so good at dating, she designed a popular singles programme, 'The Art of Flirting', which was featured in Life magazine, but still she did not meet her match.

Finally, her friend Burt gave her his advice about finding a mate: 'Just give it up to the angels, Marianna,' he told her, and gave her a cloth angel that she propped up on her windowsill as a reminder.

Marianna went on lecturing all over the world in such exotic places as Bahrain and Kuwait, appearing on programmes with the likes of Colin Powell, John Sununu, Marcia Clark and Christopher Reeve.

Something was missing in her life, though. She just wanted to, as she says, simply 'meet and marry a wonderful man'.

She kept answering personal ads but was discouraged to find that the flattering, high-sounding hyperbole in the classifieds often did not match the reality once she agreed to a date. So she was tickled to read one morning in her local California *Burlingame Gazette* a notice that was straightforward with no frills and made her hold her sides with laughter:

Breathing, has pulse, and can eat without assistance.
If you chuckled, call . . .

She liked this guy. She decided to call.

Before dialling the number, Marianna went to fill her dog's water dish. That's when she discovered that Burt's angel had fallen into the sink.

She picked up the angel and held it close.

'Surely this was a sign that the man of my dreams was on his way.'

THE MAN who placed the funny ad was named Frederick. They talked on the phone, but never met. Another dead end.

EIGHT months later, Marianna was on an aeroplane, coming back from one of her international presentations, feeling lonely. She grabbed a legal pad from her briefcase and wrote a letter to God describing the type of man she wanted.

'I wrote it in the present tense and I was very specific.' She wrote it as a prayer of thanksgiving.

> *Dear God,*
>
> *I am very thankful for my husband. He is committed 100 per cent to me, monogamous, spiritual and we laugh so much together. He is my best friend and a wonderful lover. We have wonderful sex together and we love each other deeply. We are so connected to each other mentally, spiritually, psychologically, socially, physically and intellectually. We lead a balanced life together, we are successful and happy in our careers, and we love animals. We love and trust each other completely when we are apart. Our relationship is one of ease. Playfulness. We communicate our differences easily to each other. We are sexually attracted to each other. We both want and plan to spend our lives together in marriage. Our families cherish each other. We travel together and celebrate holidays together. Thank you for my lifelong partner and best friend.*

Within a few days of her arrival home, the phone rang. It was Frederick.

'He had been cleaning his room and found my phone number behind his computer. We met and were engaged in three months, married nine months later.'

That was three years ago. Today, Marianna and Frederick enjoy exactly the kind of marriage she was grateful for in advance.

Wailing Wall

The idea of writing letters to God is no new-fangled notion.

In Jerusalem, near the Muslim Mosque of Omar, there is a fifty-nine-foot wall, believed to be a remnant of the Temple of Solomon from the tenth century B.C. In front of this wall, Jews gather on Fridays to lament and pray. Traditionally, they write messages to God, which they tuck into the crevices of the ancient holy rock. The power of these messages is so cherished that people often ask emissaries to place the notes in the wall for them.

A woman I know named Karla did that. She and her husband, Mark, were not able to conceive. A group from the Christian church they attend was going to the Holy City. Karla scratched a quick line, 'I want a baby', on a scrap of paper and asked the delegate to put it in the Wailing Wall. As Karla tells me this choice bit over the phone, I can hear her toddler playing happily in the background.

'We call Kadin our miracle child.'

WRITING letters to God, what a unique idea. And the good news is, you don't need a postbox or a stamp.

• NOW YOU •

Write letters to God of praise and thanksgiving, or write to God at night, asking questions, or for guidance in decision-making. When you wake up in the morning, let the answer come to you through your pen. Sounds bizarre, but it can't hurt.

Dear God, help me in this project.
How can I feed my family?
Do you like me, God?
Am I doing the right thing?
And by the way, have you seen the jumper I misplaced?

You will be astonished at the answers – and you will find your jumper.

16

RESISTANCE
HAS MEANING

When you find yourself hesitating before the next step in achievement of your goal, it's easy to blame the procrastination on an overworked schedule, or on other people not cooperating. Guess what? It's you who is keeping you from completion. Let's find out why.

Trina's Story

I ran into my friend Trina by chance. She was waiting for a bus on a busy street when I drove past. I invited her to join me for coffee at Vivace's and offered to give her a ride home. Since we had not seen each other in almost six months, we had a lot of catching up to do.

Trina is a vivacious, totally captivating young woman. She had recently returned from a trip to Ireland; with great merriment, she confided that she came back with a permanent souvenir: a butterfly charm dangling off a ring pierced into her bellybutton.

As we talked, she began to tell me about a dream she had and the latest developments surrounding it.

Then she showed me a Post-it note, a plain yellow 2- by 2-inch piece of paper pressed into the front page of her diary: a simple patch with a history behind it. That square heralded an adventure waiting to take place, the first step in the fulfilment of a longtime aspiration.

Trina filled me in on some background. She studied economics in college; from the first class, she was on fire with the possibilities it presented. She kept thinking that the practical application of economic principles could make a profound difference in the world.

So she took another class and started reading every book she could get her hands on that had to do with economics. The more she read, the more certain she became that she wanted to help developing nations in a concrete way, but she did not have a clue where to start. How did she get from a bachelor's degree in business to developing economic policy?

'I didn't know what avenue I would take. I knew I didn't want to get into politics and that discouraged me; I thought politics was the only way to break into policymaking.'

When she heard that the Peace Corps used business majors, she went to a Peace Corps lecture, but it turned out that it wasn't right for her, it wasn't what she wanted to do.

'Teaching or being a doctor gives immediate help, but the real problem is *money*. The poorer countries of the world don't have any sort of sustainable economy.'

Once again, Trina was discouraged, thinking an organization that did what she wanted to do didn't exist.

'I had this big dream and no practical way of carrying it out, so I gave up on it.'

MEANTIME, Trina went about her life. Her current job was assistant coordinator for the Olympic Summer Music Festival, a three-month programme of chamber music started by the Philadelphia String Quartet. She enjoyed her work and liked being part of a non-profit arts organization that was making a vital contribution to the community. But, she admitted bluntly, 'It's OK to do this now, when I'm in my twenties, but after that, what? I don't want to do this for the rest of my life.'

Trina also told me she had been volunteering at a place called Washington Works, an eight-week training programme for women on welfare to prepare them to get jobs. The course teaches them such things as secretarial skills, using a computer, handling the telephone and then helps with placement.

Trina acted as an advocate for women going through the programme. When she signed up, they paired her with a woman with three children who was twenty-six years old.

'I felt as though I learned more from her than I helped her, because she was so incredibly brave.'

In addition to her job coordinating the music festival and her volunteer work, Trina also worked in an art gallery several evenings a week. One night recently, she told me, there were no customers or viewers in the gallery. She was all alone and bored. She picked up a stray newsletter and started reading it in a cursory way. It was just a random newsletter that showed up in the gallery mail, not something she would normally read. Her eyes fell on the People on the Move section, where there was a write-up about a local woman.

The short piece highlighted the woman's recent appointment as executive director of Global Partnerships, an international non-profit organization whose mission was to stimulate economies in third-world countries using 'microlending'. They set up village banks and arranged small-scale loans to indigent women to get them started in home-based businesses.

Because of this programme, instead of living in extreme poverty, the women were able to make enough money to feed their families, get education for their children, build up their supplies and marketing and repay the loan with interest.

Trina sat up straight when she read that. Her eyes opened wide as she tried to take in the impact of that description.

'For three years, I have read books on economics in my free time; from all the stuff I've read, small solutions are better than big ones. Using small steps, looking at what a country already has and building on their strengths is what works. And apparently that is what Global Partnerships was doing: low-scale and local, rather than big changes, which later might fall apart.'

Even though all she knew about Global Partnerships at that point was no more than a few paragraphs in a throwaway newsletter, Trina could hardly contain her excitement.

'Straight away, I said, "I want to get involved in this."'

That's when she wrote down the company, the phone number, the address and the name of the new executive director on a Post-it note. She thought she would call them, ask more about what they did, see if they could send her information and ask them if she could get involved.

Sounds simple and direct enough.

'It was perfect – everything that I've wanted to do, what I imagined, without knowing such a thing as this existed.'

She slapped the sticky square into her daily planner.

Every day, day after day, Trina looked at that Post-it note staring her in the face. Each time she opened her diary to plan her day, look up a phone number, or check an appointment, it beckoned to her – but she never did anything about it.

Getting to the Crux of It

It took a lot of resistance to ignore that reminder. Every day it challenged her, but she did not call. Why did she not call?

When I asked her that question, Trina first excused herself: She was extremely busy at the gallery, with the music festival and her volunteer work. The more we talked about it, though, the more she had to admit that being busy was not what was keeping her from dialling that number. With a sigh of resignation, she acknowledged that it was only herself stopping her.

'You know what it's like, when you finally found just the right fit, and you're scared to act on it, because you worry, If I touch it, is it going to break? It is so hard to pick up the phone and call her, even though I want to talk to her so much. It is hard to do because it is exactly what I want.'

I asked Trina if she would be willing to write out her objections to get at what was underneath her inaction. I shared with her a principle I have taught for many years and believe in strongly: Resistance has meaning, and getting behind resistance, not just around it, will set you free.

Right then and there, I invited her to take out her pen and a piece of paper, to write and keep writing, peeling away the layers until she got to the core of it.

After an initial awkwardness, she was surprised at how quickly the words flowed. This is what she wrote:

> *The people working for the executive director are probably all older than me, and have tons of business background. Why would they want someone like me, someone who doesn't have much experience?*
>
> *I feel stupid calling and saying, 'Wow, I want to hear more about what you do.' I don't know what to say. I don't have that much training in economics, it's more of a gut feeling and an instinct. The big thing is I feel like I can't talk intelligently about what it is that I want to do.*

And then Trina remembered when she was in Ireland, how she went home with an Irish family for Christmas. She rode back from Clare to Dublin, three hours in the car with her friend Michael and his older brother, Adrian, who had majored in economics.

> *When I told Adrian how great it was that he majored in economics, and how I had wanted to major in economics and work on the economy in developing nations, he went off, saying, 'I don't know who you think you are, you Americans. You think that you can go to the third world and change things around when they were just fine to begin with.'*
>
> *All the way to Dublin, he was berating me. He would not let me get a word in edgewise — he was too busy telling me why everything I thought was wrong.*

In writing it out, Trina realized how much the shadow of Adrian's comments still hung over her, and how she had internalized them into her own self-doubts.

What was I going to say to her? She would think that I was a crazy young gushing girl who didn't know what she was talking about.

TRINA had a smile on her face when she finished writing. It suddenly all made sense. It felt good just to know. When you are honest, shackles drop; she felt lighthearted, as though she were putting down a heavy burden that she had been carrying on her back for a long time.

ONCE you identify the meaning behind your resistance, the block disintegrates, leaving you wide open for fulfilment. When you own the life you live, you open the way to claim the life you want.

LESS than a week after we met, Trina walked into a cocktail party honouring local dignitaries and the volunteers at Washington Works.

She started talking to a woman she knew from her committee, who, in turn, was talking to another woman. Trina introduced herself to the other woman, and asked her where she was from.

The woman smiled back at her and said, 'Well, I just got a new job. I'm the executive director of Global Partnerships, a non-profit organization.'

TRINA wasted no time in offering her services to help in any way possible.

TRINA never stopped studying, never gave up her dream to make a worldwide difference through economic principles, to help impoverished people to live decent lives, to rid the world of hunger. A scary phone call almost stopped her, until she faced foursquare the meaning behind her resistance. Then the world was free to help her along a little.

• NOW YOU •

RESISTANCE HAS MEANING.

It is an adage worth highlighting. What in your life are you resisting? Where are you digging your heels in? Write down the reasons behind your reluctance. What is it about moving forward that does not seems safe? You may think it is because of forces outside of you — pressures at work, a bank account low on funds, an unsupportive parent or partner. Go ahead. Blame it on someone else and something else. Start with that to get it out of your system. And then keep writing until you come to the truth. What is it about *you* that resists taking this next step?

The truth shall set you free, and free the world to help you along a little.

17

CREATING A RITUAL

When you attach your writing to a ceremony, it becomes somewhat sacred. Ritual recognizes something larger than yourself as part of the plan. Adding ritual to the writing of your goals makes the message more meaningful. It sets something in motion.

Elaine's Story

Elaine St James is the author of a popular series of simplicity books, including *Simplify Your Life* and *Inner Simplicity*. Having written a book a year for four years straight, she was ready to present her ideas to audiences through professional speaking, quite an accomplishment for a woman who did not, until recently, consider herself a writer and once had a fear of public speaking. A mutual friend gave her my name and she called me for advice on marketing and managing speaking engagements. We hit it off right away and soon found ourselves chatting long-distance like sisters separated at birth and now reunited.

Elaine exudes warmth and friendliness and punctuates her narratives with lighthearted laughter. She seems amazed at her own success and is clearly convinced that anyone could do what she did.

I don't remember how we got on the topic, but when Elaine started talking about a ceremony she and a friend engage in every New Year's Eve, my ears pricked up. By the time she finished explaining the details, my heart was pounding and I was determined to put it into practice myself.

The Arrow Ceremony

Here's how it started: Elaine and her friend meet every year for New Year's goal setting. About ten years ago, the friend heard about an interesting custom and they thought they would try it. Elaine has been doing it every year since.

'It goes like this: In many Native-American cultures, tribes and families would gather to start up a new year at the solstice and have a special celebration, where they would make a request to the Great Spirit to eliminate certain things that they no longer wanted in their lives, and to bring *in* things that they now wanted to have in their lives. As a way of representing this, they would craft six arrows: three to represent the things they did not want, and three for the things that they did want.'

The preparation was as important as the ceremony itself. 'They would lovingly carve these special arrows, using bird feathers for the ends of the arrows. They called them "death arrows" and "life arrows", because they held, respectively, the things they wanted to be dead and out of their lives, and those they wanted to bring life to.'

The death arrows were put in low ground, in a circle inscribed with tobacco leaves.

'One by one, they would each step into the circle from the north, put the arrows in the ground, and say certain silent prayers, concentrating on that which they were willing to give up, or what they wanted to be rid of. Once everybody had done that, they would burn those arrows. The smoke would send a signal to the Great Spirit.'

Then they would go to higher ground, inscribing a similar circle, this time leaving the opening to the south.

'Again one by one, they would go into the new circle and put the arrows in the ground, and make the request to the Great Spirit for what they wanted to bring into their lives. They would leave those arrows standing for the Great Spirit throughout the year.'

According to Elaine's friend, it was supposed to be magical, absolute magic.

'What you requested to be taken out of your life would be removed, and what you wanted to come in, came in. The Indians had unswerving faith that what they asked for would be granted if they went through this ceremony.'

Southern California Ecological Version

Elaine and her friend adapted the Native-American tradition to their own circumstances.

'We did not know how to make arrows, so the first year

we went out and got sticks – willow branches – and tied ribbons to the ends to represent the feathers.

'My friend, her two daughters and I cut six little strips of paper for each of what we called the "good arrows" and the "bad arrows". We wrote up our intentions, and then taped them to the willow branch.'

Elaine remembers that they all, including the children, took the preparation very seriously. They thought hard about the question, 'What do we want in our lives and out of our lives?' They wrote out the answers purposefully and taped them carefully to the willow branches. They had the attitude, 'It works for the Native Americans, it's going to work for us.'

THE PLAN was to get up early the next morning, because the custom was to do this ceremony before sunrise. Elaine and her friend were not scrupulous about that part.

'My friend and I got up before dawn as promised, but it was such a circus getting these young girls – ages thirteen and sixteen – up, even though they really got into it the night before.

'They were totally committed, but when it came time to get up in the morning, they were tired after staying up late doing all this preparation. So we said, "Oh well, the Great Spirit will understand an extra hour."

'We finally got them going; everyone bundled up, because it was cold, and we piled in the car and went up into the hills. We found a spot that looked right and we got out of the car and climbed over a fence. We were probably tres-passing.'

Elaine had purchased an expensive brand of tobacco and they broke it up and created a round trail of brown leaves.

'After we inscribed the circle, we went inside it and said out loud to the Great Spirit what we wanted out of our lives.'

Elaine counted on the Great Spirit to make allowances for Southern Californian environmental concerns and fire regulations as well as sleepy teenagers.

'Rather than burning those arrows, we buried them, because we live in a fire zone, where there is a burn ban. We figured instead of seeing the smoke, the Great Spirit would hear our requests, since we said them out loud.'

Then they got in the car and drove to higher ground and did the same thing with the circle opened to the south this time.

'We went into the circle and made our requests. Rather than leave these petitions standing, where someone might find them, we buried them discreetly. We figured that the Spirit could find them and grant them either way.'

Over the years, the practice evolved as Elaine made personal adjustments to the rite.

'For every year after that I got a box of number-two pencils. It was easier than locating enough willow branches and arrows are hard to come by. Also, the sharpened ends went easily into the ground.'

She continued to use colourful ribbons in place of feathers, making a special trip to the fabric store to get real ribbon.

'The ribbons were five to six inches long, about as long as the pencil, and we put them together with a piece of tape at the eraser end of the pencil – bright-coloured strips of ribbon coming out of the end of the pencil – black ribbon for the death arrows and red, yellow, green and blue for the life arrows.'

Important Enough to Pay Attention to

Putting your petitions on paper imprints them on your subconscious. Elaine says, 'If it was important enough for you to make a request, it is important enough to pay attention to.

'The ritual is profound because of everything involved in doing it. Any ritual can be profound in that way. To me, it was a new observance, so I really got into it.

'One of the reasons this particular technique is powerful is because there are so many steps involved, so many things that you have to do to energize your petitions. These steps are important, because in performing these steps, you send a message to your subconscious that says, "I am taking this seriously."

'Even the night before, preparing becomes a serious message to your subconscious.'

Quantum Leap

Elaine often copies her major requests in her journal in addition to the predawn burial.

'I don't know if the others do this, but I frequently write down what my arrows are when I come back after the ceremony.'

Sometimes the petitions read like a prayer.

'For the first couple of years, we just wrote single sentences; they got deeper and deeper as we went on. As we saw how effective they were, we got more and more and more serious – at least I did – about constructing what I wanted.'

Elaine is often amazed when she goes back and revisits those journal pages a year or so later and realizes that 'it happened without my realizing it had happened'.

One year Elaine wrote an arrow asking for guidance, for a quantum leap in financial and personal arenas, and the way to make a difference in other people's lives.

'I went on and forgot about this arrow. It wasn't until several years later that I looked back and thought, breathlessly, Wow! Look at all that happened because I made that arrow.

'I did not have a *clue* what I was asking for. I just knew I wanted to take a giant step forward in my personal and professional life.'

She is astonished now to reread this life arrow from over ten years ago:

Great Spirit,

I would like guidance in stepping on to a new plateau of personal and financial growth and achievement. I want to make a great step forward in terms of what I will accomplish with my life from this point onward. In a quiet understated way, I want to be able to make a difference in people's lives and to make a positive contribution to the world. I am just entering into the main stretch. Please help me to expand exponentially in all areas of my life.

That was January 1988. That spring, Elaine got the idea to write a real-estate book. She had not ever thought about writing a book before. She figured out how to write a proposal, figured out how to find an agent, got a publisher, started writing the book and then submitted the manuscript.

'The book was a smash hit – CNN, the works. And then I found out that Viking, the publisher, was going to send me on a tremendous tour.'

There was one problem. She was terrified of public speaking and always had been.

'I had always said to the universe, "Give me a reason to get over this fear, and I will." Now here was the reason. I had to get over my fear of public speaking in order to do the promotion.'

So she enrolled in Toastmasters, a club where members learn speaking skills, and she went on tour, in spite of her high anxiety. Soon she wasn't so scared any more. The more she did it, the less it frightened her.

As Elaine sees it now, that was the beginning step of a whole new propellant towards personal, financial and inner achievement. It took several years, but she looks back and sees how it started there.

It was because of the success of the first book that she realized how complex her life was and became determined to simplify it.

'I got back from the tour and looked at my time management system, which was the size of Nebraska – it was *huge*. I said, "This is crazy." My life was complicated. I had the book to promote, I had my own real-estate investment portfolio to manage and I had started seminars teaching agents how to do this real-estate investing technique. All of that coming together the way it did forced me to simplify, and it was out of simplifying that I wrote *Simplify Your Life* and the books that followed on the same theme. Out of that, I became a writer.'

Her first book was on equity sharing. Being a *writer* was the furthest thing from her mind.

'I only wrote the real-estate book because there wasn't one out there and I figured it would be a helpful technique. I wasn't thinking of myself as a writer; I was writing as an investor. And when I wrote *Simplify Your Life*, I wrote it because so many people were asking me, coming up to me and saying, "I hear you've simplified your life, you got rid of the big house, you got rid of all your stuff . . . I need to do that; how did you do it? What did you do?"'

Elaine made a pledge to herself that she would not do anything she did not enjoy.

'The idea came to write the simplicity book and I thought I would enjoy that, so I did it.'

The next book came as naturally.

'When I was on *Oprah*, Oprah said to me, "Elaine, what do you *do* with all this time?" And that's how *Inner Simplicity* came about. It wasn't until I was writing *Inner Simplicity*, by now my third book, that I started getting letters from people who said my second book had changed their lives. I was thrilled by the letters I got and the people I heard from. Then it finally occurred to me: Hey, I could be a writer.'

Three more *Simplicity* books followed. More than a million copies of these books have sold so far and have certainly made a profound difference in people's lives in a quiet, understated way.

'I am absolutely convinced, it is clear to me that it all came out of that life arrow with its prayer to the Great Spirit to guide my life.

'Out of that, it was writing a book, it was simplifying, it was getting over my fear of public speaking, it was getting into inner realms that I had not even *thought* about at that point.

'There is no question in my mind that it happened because I made that declaration.'

AND THERE is no question in her mind that anyone could do what she did.

It's the Motive That Matters

I first heard about Elaine St James's arrow tradition in February, a few days before my birthday. So as a birthday gift to me, my 'cohorts in crime', Dorothy and Bill, offered to go through the ceremony with me. As part of the preparation, Dorothy cooked a special meal of fresh trout, rice with cranberries and a terrific desert of lemon ginger snaps. We spent a long time devising the pencils. We got into a heated discussion of whether the ribbon-feathers should go straight up or sideways like little flags. We finally opted for the flag style because it was easier to attach, but I admit I was worried if that was correct.

We put all the black-beribboned pencils in one paper sack and the multicoloured ones in another, lest we grab and bury the wrong ones in the dark. Before retiring, we packed up a torch, a small trowel, a butane flamethrower, and a compass on a red rope.

On our way to the marina at dawn the next morning, we realized we did not have tobacco, so we stopped at an all-night convenience store. None of us had smoked since college days, so it felt funny buying Camels.

We started to fret. There was the beginning of light in the sky. Were we past predawn? Bill assured us that sunrise was at 7:10 A.M. and we still had plenty of time. Then we worried about the cigarettes: Were Camels strong enough, or would it have been better to purchase Durham loose tobacco?

When we got to the beach, we carefully inscribed a circle on the rocky sand near the water with an opening to the south, and one by one we buried the death arrows with their notations of the things we wanted to get rid of in our lives. Then we turned around, climbed over the railway tracks, and hiked high up the side of the hill, where we made a tobacco-laced circle with the opening to the north, and burned with pomp and circumstance the life arrows, inscribed with our highest aspirations.

We stood a moment silently and then suddenly, a train came rushing out of the darkness along the tracks. The unexpected power of it rooted us to the ground to keep our balance and blew our hair back. It seemed like a good, solid sign.

When we came down off the mountain top, we went to Starbucks to debrief. The sun was just starting to come up. Over steaming mugs of Yukon blend, we checked my notes from Elaine and found out, to our horror, we had it all backwards – the opening on the lower ground is supposed to point *north*, and the upper ground points *south*. In addition, we were meant to burn the former and bury the latter.

Oh no! Now we were inviting *into* our lives all the things we wanted to be liberated from, and scattering to the winds the very things we wanted an abundance of. We groaned over our coffee and wondered what to do.

When I arrived home, it was my young daughter Katherine, wiser than her years, who put my heart at ease. She dismissed all my concerns as inconsequential.

'It's the *motive* that matters, not the particulars,' she told me.

How right she was.

Katherine's comment reassured me and then made me smile. One of my black arrows had listed a trait I wanted to dispense with: worrying so much. The fact is, none of it mattered, not the direction of the ribbons or the time of day, not the brand of cigarettes or the burning or burying. The only thing that mattered was the intent and we were very clear on that. Our intent was to focus on our deepest desires, what we wanted dearly and what we no longer would tolerate, and we were appealing to something bigger than us to help us out.

Keep that in mind as you prepare your own ritual. It is not so much *what* you do as *how* you do it. Do it mindfully and with respect and you will have results.

It's not the particulars, it's the motive that matters.

• NOW YOU •

Adapt the Indian arrow tradition to your particular circumstances or design a ritual of your own. Make it as elaborate as you like, remembering that the preparation is as important as the ceremony. Include whatever creates solemnity for you. Incorporate in some form the four elements of earth, air, fire and water. Include food and some props or symbols, incense or herbs, for example. You might want to use a special writing instrument, like a handmade quill pen, cutting the tip of a goose feather to make the nib, and dipping it in bottled ink.

Adding ritual to the writing of your goals makes the message more meaningful. It sets something in motion.

18

LETTING GO, CREATING BALANCE

Besides introducing the element of ritual to writing it down and making it happen, what intrigued me about Elaine's story was the concept of 'willingness to let go'. It added a component to the process that I had not been considering.

The Native-American tradition Elaine described included not only asking for what you want of life, but also relinquishing what you do not want, what you are ready to give up. In her book *Living the Simple Life*, Elaine recommends that when you bring in something new, you throw out or give away something old. New toy for your children? Give an old one to the Salvation Army. New kitchen utensil? Throw out one you don't use. New book? Go through your shelves and pick a book to pass on to a friend. Create room for the new by letting go of what you no longer use.

Mark Victor Hansen, of *Chicken Soup for the Soul* fame, has a radical idea that I tried once and it worked. He suggests tagging with Post-it notes every piece of clothing in your wardrobe with numbers 1 to 10, with 1 being 'love it, wear it all the time' and 10 being 'I'll never wear this again unless I'm invited to a retro costume party'. Work fast on the tagging; don't stop to sentimentalize. Then go back and throw out or donate to charity or a friend (or a pre-school for dressing-up) everything higher than 3.

At first, your wardrobe will look bare (guess what? that's your core wardrobe anyway). Here's the magical part. Within a few months, your wardrobe will be full again, only this time with only 1s to 3s; in other words, it will be filled with clothes you actually wear. If you're like me, you won't even remember buying them, so it's not as though you suddenly went on a spending spree and have a big dip in your clothing budget. Instead, you look up one day and it hits you that your wardrobe is full again and you stop to sort it out: Where did all these clothes come from? Perhaps the cardigan was a gift from a friend, the trousers on sale caught your eye one day when you were out buying a present for someone else.

The point is that by being willing to throw out what was not working in your wardrobe, you surreptitiously make room for something new – and better. Something that works. The wonder is that it happens subtly, even as Mark Victor promised it would.

The analogy is clear. In life, we often need to be willing to get rid of the old, that which no longer serves us, to make room for, to prepare for the new.

Over the years, I have taken many 'human effectiveness/personal development'-type seminars. Consistently, they begin with variations on the same challenge. To answer for yourself before you even begin the work three questions, like a mythological courting test: Why did you come? What do you hope to gain? What are you willing to sacrifice? It was that last one that always got to me. I did not like the idea that I had to give up in order to get.

Now I understand the power of this principle across the board – in everything from cleaning the clutter in the attic to getting rid of relationships that no longer support you to make room for those that do.

A wise teacher once told me, 'Becoming a master means willingness to let go of whatever isn't working in your life. Letting go of the familiar is hard.'

Relinquishing what isn't working is tied to taking respons-ibility for your life.

The black arrows of the arrow ceremony, burned or buried on the low ground, thus create a balance and let you take responsibility for your life. They are a declaration to the world that you are moving out of the victim stance and taking ownership and action.

Soon after, you might find yourself changing your behav-iour in subtle ways that you do not at first realize are connected to your request.

Elaine, for example, for her book *Inner Simplicity*, came up with a visual, measurable method for combating pessimism. It is based on an ancient Chinese ritual with pebbles, but Elaine substitutes beans – one bean in a cup for each negative thought you have during the day.

'At the end of the day, look at that once-empty cup and see how many negative thoughts you've had. It's a *graphic* message to your subconscious. It's a way of tracking your mind, forcing you to get in the habit of starting to *recognize* a negative thought when it comes up.'

It took a while for Elaine to connect the black bean trick

she was recommending to others and was then doing herself with the fact that she had buried an arrow on which she had written,

I want to get rid of worry and negative thinking.

'It wasn't until I looked back and realized all the things I had done to get rid of negative thinking, like affirmations, the black bean system, and writing it out in my journal if I had a situation in my life that was creating a lot of negative thinking. Then I remembered the arrow wish.'

Reaching a Deeper Level

At first it seems like a contradiction, but sometimes the thing we need to let go of is the very thing we want. Gloria met her mate only after she began to entertain the vision of what it would be like not to have this man in her life.

'I had to be willing to not get what I most dreamed of.'

Later, she told me a story about two friends of hers who tried unsuccessfully for several years to adopt a baby. Finally, Gloria suggested to them that they do what she did and write letters to their unknown child. They did that for about a year and their writing taught them something. They came to a place of peace. They told Gloria, 'We recognized that we were a couple, a family, even without this baby.'

Three days later, they got their baby.

• NOW YOU •

1) Start with your wardrobe to give yourself an ex-
    perience of how freeing it can be to let go, as a
    visual example of how holding on to something
    no longer useful to you is standing in the way of
    making room for what you want. Armed with a
    pen and a pad of Post-its and using the approach
    described above, quickly label every garment in
    your wardrobe with a sticky note numbered 1 to
    10. Then give away or throw out any item higher
    than 3. Before you know it, you will have new
    outfits hanging there – clothes you like and actu-
    ally wear. I guarantee it.

    Let that be a lesson for your life, especially if you
    are stuck in achieving a long-term goal.

2) Write on slips of paper the things that are not
    working in your life of which you are willing to
    let go. Ceremoniously dispose of the slips, one by
    one. You could build a fire and purposefully cast
    them individually into the flames. Consign them
    to drowning – in a lake or river, over the side of
    a boat – or flush them down the toilet. (I have
    never personally done this, but a friend tells me it
    is enormously satisfying.) Perhaps you could put
    the slips inside helium balloons and let them float
    away to the sky. Release, like captured birds let out
    of their cage and sent heavenward with a blessing,
    whatever it is that is holding you back.

3) Be willing to let go of what you want. In the Hindu Scripture, the *Bhagavad Gita*, Krishna tells Arjuna that it is the surrender of attachment to results that brings serenity.

THROUGH writing you will come to that plateau of peace. Rest there for a while, for something exciting is about to happen.

19

GIVE THANKS

On our refrigerator we have a saying that has been there for many years.

If you have a dream, follow it.

If you catch a dream, nurture it.

If your dream comes true, celebrate!

CELEBRATION acknowledges the victory and gives you a chance to stop and honour those around you: family, friends and others, who helped make your dream a reality.

Celebrate the results and say thanks to the people who helped you get there.

Creating Conscious Acts of Gratitude

Stopping to say thanks completes the arc and prepares you for what's next.

Ron, the fellow who writes his 'List of Intentions' every day, shared with me a notion he learned from a friend who was studying to become a shaman. The friend told Ron to acknowledge the good happening in his own life by consciously doing kind acts for others.

When Ron got the apartment he wanted and the perfect roommate, he went out of his way to help another student who was looking for a place to stay. His friend suggested that the acts of gratitude be conscious and planned, not just random or retroactive.

Be Grateful for What You Already Have

You needn't wait to get what you want to be thankful.

Gloria told me that, in waiting for her soul mate, a turning point came for her when she was bemoaning her fate to a friend and the friend, rather than commiserating, asked her a pointed question.

'My friend Jane looked at me and said, "Why should God give you more if you are not grateful for what you have?"

'It was a powerful truth and an enlightening sentence. At that moment, I realized I needed to be grateful for my life before I could invite in my soul mate. It's all about gratitude.'

That night, Gloria wrote a letter to him:

Dear Soul Mate,
So many wonderful things have happened in the last week to help me to acknowledge my ability to positively create good in my life. I feel so blessed and wonder at this joy of creation. Of course, the ultimate miracle is to have you manifest in my life. My temp-

tation is to always deny the good and beauty and
abundance I have if you are not there – but I am
getting to see my tricks and I am changing.
Appreciation, Lord, is my mantra.

'I had to accept the blessings God had given me first
before I could receive more blessings. Thanksgiving first and
then I was open to receive again.'

My blessings are great and I am grateful.

Paying Bills with Gratitude

For many years now I have written the word 'Thanks!' on
the memo line in the bottom left corner whenever I write
out a cheque. Although I have been doing it for years, I don't
do it automatically, but deliberately. It is a way to say thanks
for the money that will come back to me, thanks that I have
the money to spend, and, most especially, thanks to the person
or company to whom I am writing out the cheque.

Writing 'Thanks!' on the memo line is a reminder of all
the people who make my life easier.

It is a way of taking a moment to think about the service
the cheque is for and the people behind the purchase. It
makes me stop and think, Thank you for providing my
groceries, for keeping my house warm, for collecting my
rubbish, and giving me a recycling can. Thank you for equip-
ping the phone lines so I can run my business and stay in
touch with people I love.

When I write 'Thanks!' on the memo line, I can sit down
to pay my bills with a grateful heart.

Making the World a More Pleasant Place

My sons, James and Peter, take this 'attitude of gratitude' one step further; they send out a slew of personal thank-you notes every day.

I mentioned earlier that together they own and operate a graphic design firm. They started small, a two-man operation at the kitchen table and now they have a huge downtown office with staff and large accounts.

Peter says, 'No matter how big we get, no matter how much money we make, how many employees we hire, we never forget the people who helped us get where we are.'

It is common practice in business to give gifts to clients, to the people who are giving you money; for example, a manufacturer's rep might bring tins of popcorn at the end of the year to thank the distributor; he appreciates that they are buying from him and selling his product. Peter tells how they add to that.

'Bullseye Graphics remembers clients, of course, but we also remember the vendors – the people who are doing a job for us – not just the people who pay us, but the people we pay. We have a motto: "Take care of the people who take care of you."'

So Peter and James write thank-you notes to the people who do a job for them. They drop a card along with payment to the photographer who recently spent two hours out in the cold with them for a shoot, or send a note to the digital colour specialist at the copy shop after he worked with them into the wee hours of the morning to produce colour copies for a mock-up.

And they never pay a bill without a handwritten note

of thanks enclosed, even if it's just a routine monthly payment.

'The writing does not have to be award-winning documentation, just a simple note, a quick line dashed off and put in with the bill payment. It can be as simple as, "Thanks for helping make us look good" or "Thanks for all your hard work". Even if it says the same thing every time, it's still a day brightener for the recipient.'

Peter and James send out thank-yous to friends and family, too. There is not one of us who has not received a hand-written note for what others might think a verbal thank-you sufficed. Recently their friend Kevin asked his father-in-law, Gary, if they could borrow his truck to transport some cases of promotional material to a client.

Kevin told Gary, 'Don't be surprised if you get a thank-you note.'

As it turned out, they needed a larger vehicle, but sure enough, the next time Gary went to drive his truck, there was a note to him from James and Peter waiting in the front cab.

'Well,' says James, 'he went to all the trouble of cleaning it out and filling it with gas and being willing to let us use it, and we wanted him to know we appreciated that.'

It causes a kind of chain reaction; people they do business with are pleased to see them, and then in turn are nice to other customers, maybe even writing a note themselves to someone. And because they write out their thanks, James and Peter are more aware of the good things happening in their world and the support they get all around. They emphasize the positive and don't take people for granted.

An attitude like that spills over. As James puts it, 'You

start noticing and acknowledging little courtesies, like giving a wave in traffic when someone lets you in or lets you pass.'

Peter grins and says, 'We are making the world a more pleasant place, one thank-you note at a time.'

• NOW YOU •

1) Fill a page with all the blessings in your life. I am grateful for _____ . . . and keep on going. Make it a litany. Start with the small and obvious.

> *I am grateful for my friends.*
> *I am grateful for the roof over my head.*
> *I am grateful for libraries.*
> *I am grateful for my jumper, which keeps me warm.*
> *I am grateful for sunsets and rainbows.*

It's OK to go more than a page if your pen starts running away with you.

2) Look for ways to thank people in writing; for example, fill out the customer comment form in the post office; not to file a complaint about misdirected mail, but a compliment about a clerk who was particularly helpful and cheerful.

When you shop or do business with a company, get the name of the person whose service you appreciated and put your appreciation in writing.

3) When your dream comes true, celebrate! Make that celebration include conscious acts of kindness towards others. And be sure to thank all those who helped you on your way.

When you remember to say thanks, when you live your life in a spirit of gratefulness, life will present you with even more things for which to be grateful.

20

HANDLING BREAKDOWN

What if you write it down and it doesn't happen?

The first thing to stop and consider is, maybe it *did* happen! Maybe it just did not happen the way you intended. Go back and look at the outcome of the outcome, the benefit of the benefit of the benefit. What was it that you wanted out of that goal? You may have got what you wanted after all, from a different avenue.

MY FRIEND Charlie wanted to go to medical school. She wrote it down, described it in detail – and did not get in. Did she fail?

She wanted to go to medical school so she could become a doctor. She wanted to be a doctor so she could help people who were sick. Charlie now works in a large city hospital as a physician's assistant helping people with AIDS.

Another friend of mine applied for a job he really wanted.

He wrote on successive mornings how having that job would change his life. He did not get the job.

'At first,' he told me, 'I felt embarrassed to go back and reread the stuff about how much I wanted that position. Then I realized that the message over and over, clear as a bell, was not the job itself, but what it represented to me: the ability to easily pay my son's college tuition, to pay the mortgage on my house, to have the money to take a trip with my family. Those were the biggies that kept coming up in my writing, and to be satisfied in my work and feel appreciated.

'I look back now and see I got everything I wanted and some in the position I did secure; in fact, it's even better, because it's closer to my house and I like the company more. Until I realized that, I was still hung up on the fact that I wrote it down and did not get the first job.'

It wasn't the *job* he coveted; it was the security and the money that he wanted and the time to be with his family.

JAIMÉE wants to go to New York – she writes that down as the first outcome: The goal is to live and work in New York. As she continues to write, delving into the outcome of the outcome and beyond, she fills in the progression. The reason she wants to go to New York is to sing in a jazz club and she wants to do that to feel fulfilled, to do what she knows she is good at, and therefore make a contribution to the world with her talents. Because of that, she can be happy when she goes to bed at night and because of that, she'll know in her heart for the rest of her life that she can dream big and have those dreams come true.

She writes down her goal and a year later, she still has

not gone to New York. But guess what she did do? She made a demo tape to circulate to local clubs in her hometown and started singing in jazz clubs there.

She has not given up her dream of going to New York, but meantime, she can still have the outcome of the outcome in her life.

Explore Other Avenues of Attainment

There are many roads to the mountain's summit, but the view from the top is the same. When you focus on the outcome, you needn't get discouraged. You just keeping asking, 'If not that, then what? What else can I do to get the same end results?'

Humorist Marianna Nunes presents this useful formula for the 'two steps forward, one step back' dance of life:

SW. SW. SW? NEXT!

When some action you take towards a goal does not have the expected result, rather than lose heart, make it your mantra:

Some will.
Some won't.
So what?
Next!

Shift Brain Strengths

The right side of the brain traditionally governs the feeling, non-verbal part of you, while the left hemisphere handles rational thought and logic. When your goal is not working, determine which side you are operating from and make a conscious shift to the other.

Get an emotional anchor if your practical side is running the show – and running your dreams into the ground. Write about how it *feels* to achieve this goal: get passionate and expressive, attach an emotional connection.

Conversely, do something concrete if your feelings are running away with you. If your emotions (fear, doubt, worthlessness) are bringing you down, get practical. Think with your head instead of your heart. Educate yourself; get some brochures or books showing pictures of what you want looks like; talk to those who have done what you want to do; then write about some practical aspect of it to get grounded.

Shifting puts you back in charge and creates the balance to get you unstuck.

Steady On

OK. You wrote about the perfect relationship and you met someone who fitted the description completely. Then it all fell apart. Is that a failure?

You didn't get to go on the Caribbean cruise after all. Somebody else won the trip to Paris.

Try again.

Enter to win the contest again or find another to enter. That is what Helen Hadsell would tell you. Helen wrote the book *Name It and Claim It*.

I like that title.

For Helen, *Name It and Claim It* refers specifically to contests. I would extend that title to encompass anything you write down to make happen. Name it, then claim it, is what writing it down to make it happen is all about.

Helen says, 'There is no failure, only a delay in results.'

That's one for those of you who like to hand-letter plaques, sew counted cross-stitch samplers, or photocopy pithy statements to put above your computers or tuck them into the corners of your mirror.

THERE IS NO FAILURE; ONLY A DELAY IN RESULTS.

Helen goes on to explain, 'Don't ever dismiss or nullify good, positive energy because you are disappointed. Acquire the attitude, "I guess I need a little more patience." It really does wonders for your peace of body, mind and well-being.'

One of the tenets of neurolinguistic programming is that there is no such thing as failure, only feedback.

And patience is power.

Three Feet from the Gold

Napoleon Hill tells this memorable story in his classic, *Think and Grow Rich*.

A certain Mr Darby had a gold mine in Colorado during the Gold Rush. It served him well for a short while and then apparently dried up. He drilled a little further, dug a little deeper, but nothing. So he gave up and sold the mining tools and the land to a prospector for a few hundred dollars. Within *three feet* of the place where Darby stopped drilling, the new owner tapped into a gold vein worth millions.

The incident changed Darby's life. He never forgot his mistake in stopping only three feet from the gold. Years later, he said, 'That experience was a blessing in disguise. It taught me to *keep on keeping on*, no matter how hard the going may be, a lesson I needed to learn before I could succeed in anything.'

'One of the most common causes of failure,' concludes Hill, 'is the habit of quitting when one is overtaken by *temporary defeat*.'

Don't stop three feet from the gold.

Go back and dig some more.

Breakdown? Hooray!

I have some good news for you.

When everything is falling apart, it is a good sign that everything is about to come together.

In the very act of our birth, we get a lesson for life. The ten minutes before delivery is often the hardest part of labour for mother and baby. It's called 'transition'. The mother is about to give up (too late!) while the father, who has read the birthing books and taken the ante-natal classes, is ecstatic: He knows that after the long period of labour the baby is almost here.

Likewise in life, chaos often comes close to completion. When you recognize this pattern, you rejoice when everything breaks down; you must be getting close to the finishing line.

When everything falls apart, I say, 'Hooray! We must be almost done.' The computer crashes, the car's transmission goes out – wow! Something *big*, really *big* is about to happen.

Push on. The breakdown heralds completion. You are three feet away from the gold.

And if you are headed in the right direction, all you need to do is keep on walking – and keep on writing it down to make it happen.

EPILOGUE

As life would have it, in the very process of writing this book, I was enmeshed in testing the power of its principles. You remember in the introduction how faith in St Joseph helped me sell my house – well, good work – now I had to buy another to move to.

I'd like to be able to tell you that I never for a minute doubted I would find exactly what I wanted, but that would not be so. Now I look back and see. I was scared.

Of course, I wrote down what I wanted, put a 'due date' on it, yet even as I wrote it, I felt foolish and doubting. Why couldn't I be like Sydne, I thought? Write a list, pick up the newspaper, wing a prayer to 'make it easy' and get the house I wanted in the first try out the door. I found myself thinking of Gloria who confessed at one point that she felt desperate enough to grab at any man – when I got discouraged, I thought I would leap at any house even close to what I wanted.

Good houses seemed few and far between. I prayed I

would find my house in that small opening right after listing.

And I wrote letters to God; in the beginning, gentle and optimistic,

> *I thank you Lord in advance for the blessing of my new house which is oh so fine. It is waiting for us now just as surely as Ted and Gloria were meant to come together. Thank you God for Gloria, and for my new house.*

But as the weeks rolled on, the tone of the letters changed.

> *How can I take that place I saw yesterday when it does nothing for me; it feels so practical – what about the sense I've dreamed of, the sense of coming home – am I holding out? DEAR GOD WON'T YOU HELP ME HERE DON'T MAKE IT SO HARD – I'VE GOT A BOOK TO WRITE.*

Here's what I wanted in a house, what I was holding out for,

> *My new house will be sunny all around. There will be a hot tub (that's number 1). My new house has a fireplace and a cosy, creative feel and a low-maintenance, but rustic and picturesque garden.*

I even put it out there on a Life Arrow, and wrote out the 'outcome of the outcome'.

Not just a fireplace, but a

> *fireplace to tell tall tales by, and for my Egyptian scribe to guard.*

and the hot tub was

for soaking and relaxing and for entertaining friends.

I wanted it sunny

so I can write at the kitchen table in my pyjamas with a steaming cup of coffee in hand, looking out the window to the lush garden.

Generally, I wanted it to be

a place where people feel welcome, even before I've fed them.

My friends, out of kindness, urged me to be more realistic. They said, 'You'll never get the hot tub; forget the second bathroom.'

I got depressed. Nothing looked right.

One Saturday, I spent the afternoon house-hunting with my close and dear friend, Dorothy. Dorothy was enthusiastic about several places, but nothing clicked for me. I felt frozen, paralysed, shut down. It looked bleak.

That night, Dorothy's husband and my friend, Bill, called me and left a voice message. He said, 'I heard you were looking at houses with Dorothy today, and you were upset because you hadn't found anything. Give me a call; I want to talk to you.'

It was kind of Bill to phone me. I knew he was worried about me because I was so down. I truly thought he was going to gently suggest that I see a doctor and get on Prozac – or at least go to the health store and get some St John's

Wort. I felt a little defensive, ready to tell him that my depression was 'situational' rather than 'clinical'. Instead, what he said surprised me. And touched me.

Bill didn't give me advice or scolding or serious-sounding analysis of my despair. He didn't try to talk me out of my wish list or tell me to lower my expectations. He did not tell me to be realistic.

He simply said, 'I wanted to tell you that when Dorothy and I were looking for a house – it was sixteen years ago, but I still remember it clearly – it was a stressful time for us too.'

I felt suddenly relieved. The tension eased out of my body – just to know that I was not alone, that someone had walked down this path before me and understood.

I kept thinking, what Bill just did for me, I want my book to do for my readers. To know that others have gone before you, and done what you want to do – and sometimes, they too got scared and depressed and thought it wouldn't work. And they kept on believing and moving forward, even if they took one step back for every two steps forward.

That's why I wanted you to meet Marian and Sydne and Marc and Janine. That's why Gloria lets you read her very personal love letters, and why Elaine hopes that you will put the arrow ceremony into practice in your own way. They want to say to you, don't minimize your dreams and don't lose heart – if I can do this, so can you. It's OK to be scared. Do it anyway.

Bill called on Sunday morning. That afternoon, I found my house. Before 10 P.M. that very night, I had made an offer.

And now I am sitting at the kitchen table of my new cosy home with the manuscript spread out in front of me and a latte in hand, listening to Jean-Pierre Rampal on the stereo and the wind chimes in the yard, looking out the window at the rose garden and the hanging baskets of azaleas and pansies and geraniums. My Egyptian scribe, papyrus scroll on his lap and stylus in hand, with kohl-lined eyes as wise as eternity, sits on my hearth.

Pardon me while I take a break and go soak in my hot tub.

THANKS
AND
EVER THANKS

Shipwrecked Sebastian in Shakespeare's *Twelfth Night* is flab-
bergasted at the outpouring of love and attention he receives
from the sea captain Antonio, who offers to escort him
through the rough and inhospitable streets of sixteenth-
century Illyria. Sebastian protests:

'I can no other answer make but thanks/And thanks; and
ever thanks.'

His flustered sentiment echoes my own incredulity and
humble gratitude at the outpouring of love and support
guiding me through the sometimes perilous path of writing
a book. I can no other answer make but thanks and thanks
and ever thanks. First to my family: they are there for me
in so many big and little ways. Nothing brings me greater
joy than having, as my aunt Mary used to name it, 'all my
chickadees around the table'; they bring light and laughter
into my home with their grinning, handsome, wholesome
faces. The bond my children share with me, and with each
other, is a sterling thing; we would each give our lives for
the other. In the making of this book, they have been

tremendously supportive in both word and deed, not just lip service, but hands-on help.

So thank you, cuddlesome Katherine, for the velvet-foam lattes (you are the best home espresso maker in the world, my sweet). Wise beyond her years, eyes that shine with goodness, filled with grace and graciousness that puts others instantly at ease, Katherine never wavered in her belief of me. Not once, not ever.

And thanks to my energetic, charismatic Emily, full of spirit. Your luxurious laughter lights up my day. You cannot be in Emily's presence for long without soon feeling happy. Emily understands by her own life the value of hard work, yet makes life a game. She made me huge puzzle signs; I got to connect the dots for every hour spent working on a chapter, spelling out secret messages. Emily kept me going by packing my lunches with glowing notes, pushing me to persevere ('You go, girl. We are waiting for you at the finishing line'). Thanks, love.

And ever thanks to my sons James and Peter: creative, fun-loving, enormously loyal, fiercely proud of each other; fearless, confident and inspiring.

James, thanks for listening, even late at night, and offering masterful design and technical support; for chasing the FedEx truck with me through winding city streets, and then taking me for a margarita to celebrate completion.

Peter, your good nature puts a smile on my face which can't be erased. Thanks, Peter, for letting me bounce ideas off you, and for all the careful hours spent formatting and preparing the manuscript for submission. And thanks to dear Carolyn, Peter's bride, and my new daughter-in-love, for her affectionate, affirming way of showing how she cares, and for her ready sympathy. (She is the first to say, 'Awwwwwww' when a good 'Awwwwww' is needed.)

Nancy Ernst kept me alive through her extraordinary e-mails. Although far away, her encouragement sustained me with daily doses of kind and clever words. Dorothy and Bill Harrison fed me spiritually and actually; seems that there was always room at their table and in their hearts for me. They nourished me unconditionally.

Rhea Rolfe, thanks for answering all my questions with compassion, and shifting my perspective; cousin Mary Edna Meeks, I loved your funny 'hang in there' cards and appreciated knowing that the prayer rug was always out. Thanks to my friend Erich Parce for offering me his Powerbook when my own crashed, and for standing by with ever-ready Mac advice. Jack Meeks, thanks for telling me I could call collect, any time, night or day. Bob McChesney, my mentor and friend, you taught me to meditate, and to believe, and I am grateful. With Bob, anything is possible.

Alan Rook, thanks for the cheery wake-up calls (sometimes singing ones) and for often asking, with sincerity, 'How's the book coming?' and waiting for a reply.

For the Divine Diva herself, Laurie Cheeley, for letting me hang out in Diva's Espresso for hours on end, nursing a single tall foamy, and for having an almost psychic ability to know what I needed – when to push, when to listen. Like Miss Prothero to the firemen in their shining helmets, she said the right thing, always. And to Diva espresso maker Brady Snyder for his sunny smiles and for taking me behind the bar to instruct me in the proper technique for steaming milk.

David Schomer for his passion about coffee and his dedication to making Vivace's Roasteria a 'third place', an urban coffeehouse where people convene comfortably across socio-economic lines and share ideas in a generous space. I spend so many hours at Vivace's, David calls it my 'office'; once he even gave me his fax machine number for incoming messages. And where would I be without the coffee makers at Vivace's who start my day with a friendly greeting, pull a perfect shot, and remember the twist of orange in my drink? Thanks Dan, Paul, Jodi, Robin, Leslie, Linda, Cozy, Mark, Cindy, Stephanie, Holly, Mary, Wade (ask him about his young son Aiden if you want to see a dad glow). You make me feel welcome.

I LEARNED a new word recently: 'lagniappe' (lan-yap). It is a Creole expression, originating with Louisiana shopkeepers' tradition of throwing in something extra with your purchase, the unexpected thirteenth doughnut. In the wonderful world of book publishing, I have been gifted with lagniappes, more than I could have dreamed of or anticipated. So thanks and ever thanks to sharp and witty Jane Dystel, a firecracker of an agent; to Michele Tofflemire for her dedication in assembling a dynamite web page; to Trish Todd and Cherise Grant, my editors: you spun my head around, and did the seemingly impossible: let me keep my own author's voice while challenging me to change. With gratitude, I pay you the highest compliment: you care about this work as much as I do, and because of you, it is a better book. Thank you.

Thanks to Pat Eisemann, Director of Publicity, for sharing the vision, making me laugh in recognition, and connecting on a deep personal level. It was Pat who first taught me about 'lagniappes'. You are yourself one, Pat. A bonus, a prize.

In addition, I am grateful to each and every one of you who let me in on your lives, and let me tell your profound and powerful stories here so that others might learn and live fully alive, as you do.

Thank you, gentle Marian Sorenson, fearless Janine Shinkoskey Brodine, vivacious Trina Wintch, wise Gloria Lanza-Bajo, provocative John Sexton, unsuppressable Jaimée Cheeley, bouncy Maria Toro, brave Karla Reimers, bold Nan, daring Marianna Nunes, generous Elaine St James, effervescent Sydne Johansen, brilliant Ron Cyphers, and finally, my new life-long friend, spirit-filled Marc Acito, who constantly challenges me, and through his example, encourages me not to be afraid to touch the divine in my own life.

WE NEED guides like Antonio in our lives, sea captains to steer us on land and on water.

This book could not exist without these people. It is our gift to you.

BIBLIOGRAPHY

RHJ. *It Works!* North Hollywood, DeVorss & Company: 1926. Order by writing to DeVorss and Company, P.O. Box 550, Marina del Rey, CA, 902940550.

Allen, James. *As A Man Thinketh*. DeVorss & Company: 1979.

Bristol, Claude M. *The Magic of Believing*. New York, Simon & Schuster: 1948.

Cameron, Julia with Mark Bryan. *The Artist's Way*. London, Pan Books: 1995.

Day, Laura. *Practical Intuition*. London, Vermillion: 1997.

Hadsell, Helen. *Contesting: The Name It and Claim It Game*. Largo, Florida, Top of the Mountain Publishing: 1971. Revised 1988.

Hill, Napoleon. *Think and Grow Rich*. Original copyright, 1937; revised edition London, Thorsons: 1970.

Huang, Al Chungliang and Jerry Lynch. *Thinking Body, Dancing Mind*. New York, Bantam: 1992.

Keyes, Ken, Jr. *the hundredth monkey*. Coos Bay, Oregon, Vision Books: 1982. (Currently out of print)

Klauser, Henriette Anne. *Put Your Heart on Paper*. New York, Bantam: 1995.

Klauser, Henriette Anne. *Writing on Both Sides of the Brain*. San Francisco, HarperCollins: 1987.

Schwartz, David J., Ph.D. *The Magic of Thinking Big*. New York, Simon & Schuster: 1959.

Sher, Barbara. *Wishcraft: How to Get What You Really Want*. New York, Ballantine Books: 1979.

ABOUT THE AUTHOR

HENRIETTE ANNE KLAUSER, PH.D., is the president of Writing Resources and author of the popular books *Writing on Both Sides of the Brain* and *Put Your Heart on Paper*. Dr Klauser has taught at the University of Washington, Seattle University, California State University, University of Lethbridge (Canada) and Fordham. She addresses national associations and leads workshops for corporations on topics of goal setting, writing and relationship building. Her business clients include Fortune 500 companies like Boeing, Weyerhaeuser, Xerox, Hershey Foods, Armstrong World Industries and International Data Group (publishers of *MacWorld*). Her international workshops include presentations in Canada; Cairo, Egypt; London, England; and the island of Skyros in Greece. She has recently been invited to join a delegation to China of international leaders in communication.

Henriette has a special devotion to St Joseph Cupertino, who taught her to approach life with an attitude of belief that what you pray for will, in fact, happen. She is the mother of four remarkable children and lives in Edmonds, Washington.

You may contact Henriette by writing to:

Henriette Anne Klauser, Ph.D.
Writing Resources
P.O. Box 1555
Edmonds, WA 98020
USA

or e-mail: henriette@aol.com
website: www.henrietteklauser.com

SIMON & SCHUSTER
A VIACOM COMPANY

UNTIL TODAY!

Daily Devotions for Spiritual Growth and Peace of Mind

Iyanla Vanzant

'Iyanla Vanzant has been down and out. Now her books
are pulling others up'
Washington Post

Bestselling author Iyanla Vanzant has had an amazing and difficult
life – one of great challenges that unmasked her wonderful gifts and
led to wisdom gained. Now, in the inspiring tradition of *Acts of
Faith* – a publishing phenomenon with almost 1 million copies in
print – *Until Today!* provides a year's worth of daily inspirational
quotes, explanations from Iyanla, and brief exercises or actions for
readers to perform. *Until Today!* is a meaningful but bite-sized foray
into a deeper, more satisfying spiritual and emotional life.

PRICE £14.99
ISBN 0 684 84137 1

POCKET
B O O K S

IN SEARCH OF STONES

A pilgrimage of faith, reason and discovery

M. Scott Peck, M.D.

The work of M. Scott Peck has had a profound effect on the
lives of millions of readers and now he has produced 'the closest
thing to an autobiography' he will ever write. *In Search of Stones* is,
on the surface, the story of a three-week trip through the British
countryside that Dr Peck took with his wife Lily – looking for the
ancient megalithic stones that became an obsession for them. But
the search for stones is a search for meaning and romance and, ulti-
mately, an exploration of our own life journey . . .

In Search of Stones is a beautiful book of spirituality and quest,
faith and mystery, and the most intimate book to come from one of
our most distinguished thinkers.

PRICE £7.99
ISBN 0 671 00476 X

POCKET
BOOKS

CHOCOLATE FOR A WOMAN'S SOUL

Kay Allenbaugh

'I couldn't put it down . . . do yourself a favour by reading this book'
Jack Canfield, co-author of *Chicken Soup for the Soul*

Treat yourself to 77 true stories that celebrate life and capture the essence of what it means to be a woman. Like chocolate, these stories soothe, satisfy and delight – better yet, they are good for you!

Here are heartfelt insights on commitment, compassion, work, marriage, friendship, motherhood, love, courage, spirituality, passion and dozens of other topics.

Like a box of chocolates, this book can be enjoyed in one sitting or you can pick out treats at random and savour them one at a time. Whether you want a good laugh or need a good cry, the perfect 'chocolate story' is right here, waiting for you.

PRICE £6.99
ISBN 0 684 83217 8

SIMON & SCHUSTER

A VIACOM COMPANY

CHANGE YOUR LIFE WITHOUT GETTING OUT OF BED

The Ultimate Nap Book

SARK

International bestselling author and artist, SARK offers a guide to achieving health, wealth, and well-being through the simple joy of naps. An experienced napper herself, SARK shows how a good nap can make you more deluxe, creative, sexy, funny, intriguing, and flexible. Conjuring up the hours of 'quiet time' we all remember from childhood, she suggests great places for napping, provides instructions for indulging in fantasy naps, and offers a host of good excuses for taking a nap.

'Funny, delicious, and wise . . . Sark makes a gloomy day sunny'
Barbara Sher

PRICE £6.99
ISBN 0 684 85930 0